A
GOD
IN
NEED
OF
HELP

A play in two acts
(or five, if you think about it)

Sean Dixon

Coach House Books, Toronto

first edition

 Canada Council   Conseil des Arts
for the Arts   du Canada   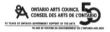 ONTARIO ARTS COUNCIL   CONSEIL DES ARTS DE L'ONTARIO   Canadä

Published with the generous assistance of the Canada Council for the
Arts and the Ontario Arts Council. Coach House Books also acknowledges
the support of the Government of Canada through the Canada Book Fund
and the Government of Ontario through the Ontario Book Publishing
Tax Credit.

LIBRARY AND ARCHIVES CANADA CATALOGUING IN PUBLICATION

Dixon, Sean, author
    A God in need of help / Sean Dixon.

A play.
Issued in print and electronic formats.
ISBN 978-1-55245-291-2

    I. Title.

PS8557.I97G63 2014   C812'.54   C2013-907686-7

Also available as an ebook: ISBN 978 1 77056 381 0.

Purchase of the print version of this book entitles you to a free digital
copy. To claim your ebook of this title, please email sales@chbooks.com
with proof of purchase or visit chbooks.com/digital. (Coach House Books
reserves the right to terminate the free download offer at any time.)

*This play is dedicated to Katerina Cizek, my wife,
who introduced me to her mother's magic Prague
and her father's scientific Prague.*

*And to Ana Fratnik, the Slovenian driver
who did not give up on me when I was lost in the Alps.*

PLAYWRIGHT'S NOTE

I spent the first days of September 2009 in Prague, visiting my father-in-law in the city of my marriage. On the tenth of September, I boarded a train heading to Ljubljana, Slovenia, a city just north of the Adriatic Sea, where my wife, Kat, was teaching a class of young documentary filmmakers right on the coast. I changed trains in Salzburg and ended up sharing the first-class car of a vintage train with four elderly women who were unable to discover a single thing about me, despite their curiosity being piqued by the porter, who had told them that my point of origin was Prague. But I didn't speak German and I didn't speak Serbo-Croatian.

I also was clueless about how the geography of Europe worked. Despite having a working knowledge of the politics and history of most of its countries, I didn't know their locations. All I knew was that Ljubljana was south of Prague and that, when I arrived, I was going to be surprisingly close to the city of Venice. That's what Kat had told me: Ljubljana was close to Venice. Who knew that the countries of the former Yugoslavia were so close to Italy? Not me.

South of Salzburg we hit some crazy beautiful mountains – as if the Rockies had been civilized, at least in places. Other places they were like the Rockies unadorned. I assumed they were the Alps, but I had neglected (as always) to look at a map, so I wasn't completely sure. And I suppose I didn't want to ask my companions in the car because I wanted to remain mysterious to them. I kept my nose in a book about the history and culture of Prague, a post–Prague Spring elegy mourning the Soviet rout of a mystical city, written in dense, mournful, poetic prose by a crazy Italian named Angelo Maria Ripellino. I was reading it for the second time.

The mountains got higher and higher and more and more beautiful. I became more and more certain I was in the Alps. I want to say I was certain, to give myself just a little bit of credit, but I really wasn't. We passed high above a town called Bad Gastein and then just pulled into its train station, as if the station were at ground level and not hovering up there in the clouds.

As we pulled out of the station, where it was sunny and beautiful, I read the following sentence in Ripellino's book:

> To prevent damage to *Das Rosenkranzfest*, the Dürer canvas his agents had bought in Venice, the Emperor had the painting carried across the Alps by four powerfully built men.

And then we plunged into a tunnel. When we came out the other end, the mountains were above us and it was raining. A few minutes later, the mountains were below us again.

It was far from ordinary to get my location on the surface of the globe confirmed by an anecdote from an obscure book written in the 1970s about a little-known event that took place in 1606. It made the mountains suddenly very real to me. It made Europe finally concrete to me, the countries all dropping into their proper places. It also made the mountains of four centuries past tangible to me, the labours of four strong Venetian men circa 1606 becoming visceral.

Earlier, I had read another sentence in that book about that same king, Rudolf (who was a shy, pudgy little man who collected art and alchemists, and whose great-grandmother on both his mother's and his father's side was Joanna the Mad of Spain). The sentence was a quote from Max Brod (the guy who swore to Kafka on Franz's deathbed that he'd burn all his works but then published them instead), describing Rudolf as being like 'a god in need of help.' I began to conceive a story about a different god, in need of a different kind of help.

Over the course of the next year, I could not find the heart of what I wanted to write about. I successfully imagined many hardships and epiphanies for my four strongmen, got to know them well, but failed to locate my own geographic point – my Alps – to make these characters fall into place. Still, because the moment of inspiration had been so strong, the sense of the men so visceral, the desire remained. I had a reading with some friends in September 2010 and the play fell flat. Still, the desire remained. A few weeks later I gave up writing it, in disgust. I told myself I would return to it in three years.

Then, six months later, while lying on a beach on the east coast of Mexico, the key to my story drifted up into my mind. I had to set the play after the fact, so I could separate my characters and show how radically different were their versions of the events. The play was about belief, and the immutable ways in which we see the world due to our philosophies, our theologies, our simple perceptions. I would never have got to that point of epiphany without that first spark of inspiration in the mountains. The path from the one to the other was my own journey on foot through the Alps.

Sean Dixon
April 2014

PRODUCTION HISTORY

A God in Need of Help had its world premiere on April 23, 2014, at the Tarragon Theatre in Toronto. The cast and crew were as follows.

Marco: Alden Adair
The Captain: Dmitry Chepovetsky
Zen: John Cleland
Borromeo: Greg Ellwand
Cocco: Daniel Kash
Dolfin: Tony Nappo
Rafal: Jonathan Seinen
Guards: Daniel Giverin and Ben Irvine

Director: Richard Rose
Set and Costume Design: Camellia Koo
Lighting Design: Kimberly Purtell
Sound Design: John Gzowski
Stage Manager: Kristen Kitcher
Assistant Director: Peter Pasyk
Fight Director: John Stead
Apprentice Stage Manager: Marc Benson
Script Coordinator: Wesley J. Colford

DRAMATIS PERSONAE

(Renier) Zen: Magistrate for the Republic of Venice

(Federico) Borromeo: Cardinal Archbishop of Milan

Marco (Chodeschino): oarmaker, strongman

(Pompeo) Dolfin: actor, strongman

(Benasuto) Cocco: retired soldier, strongman *who carried the painting*

Rafal: a young man of seventeen years or so

Captain: mercenary, Landsknecht soldier, in the employ of
   Rudolf II, Holy Roman Emperor

Guards

ACT ONE, SCENE ONE

(*Venice, Summer 1606. Council chambers in the Doge's castle. A judge – Renier Zen – presides. Beside him stands a man in the robes of a prelate: Federico Borromeo, Cardinal Archbishop of Milan. Next to them stands a mounted canvas, covered in a sheet. Venetian guards are posted at the doors. Four seeming prisoners are led to the centre and the cloaks removed from their heads, revealing them to be three powerfully built men – Dolfin, Marco, Cocco – and one seventeen-year-old boy – Rafal. A Landsknecht Captain is also present, cruelly bound. His uniform is dirty and torn, but one can still perceive the improvised ostentation characteristic of his mercenary brotherhood. Zen is consulting some papers.*)

ZEN: Gentlemen, you have been called before the magistrate for the Republic of Venice, granted the authority to represent the Council in matters of state security. I believe you all know why you're here. However, formality dictates a review.

MARCO: I am a ... simple ...

ZEN: But first you must swear an oath never to reveal what took place here, or even that you were here at all.

MARCO: But I ...

ZEN: Marco Chodeschino, oarmaker, strongman, swear!

MARCO: I swear!

ZEN: Pompeo Dolfin, actor, alchemist-assistant, snake-handler, strongman, swear!

DOLFIN: I swear!

ZEN: Benasuto Cocco, soldier, assassin, strongman, swear.

COCCO: I s-s–

ZEN: Yes, yes.

COCCO: I s–

ZEN: Boy named Rafal, no last name given and I refuse to call him a strongman when he's barely of age, there's much that is funny about him and he's a scrawny –

MARCO: Leave the boy alone.

ZEN: – he's a scrawny little foreigner to boot –

MARCO: I said LEAVE THE BOY ALONE!

(It takes all the guards to restrain him. Finally, the boy puts his hand on Marco's shoulder and calms him.)

ZEN: Rafal, boy, swear.

RAFAL: I swear.

ZEN: *(to the fettered Captain)* And the Landsknecht Captain, who accompanied them, who was supposed to guard them.

CAPTAIN: *(mumbles something)*

ZEN: Very well. It's a shameful moment for the Republic of Venice when a distinguished foreign monarch asks us to perform a simple task and we bungle it.

COCCO: With resp-pect, C-c-c-ouncillor, the t-t-t-task was n-not simple.

ZEN: If only because the wrong men were chosen for the job.

COCCO: B-b-b-b–?

ZEN: In the name of all that is serene and noble in our city, would you please close your mouth and keep it closed? Must our dignity endure the stammering of an imbecile?

It has become clear, however, that this is no longer the simple blunder that I perceive with such painful acuity. Fifty-six people have sworn that a miracle has taken place, somewhere in the middle of the Alps – the village of Pusterwald. Since I do not believe in miracles, I have little choice but to recuse myself in favour of a representative from the Roman Church: Federico Borromeo, Cardinal Archbishop of Milan, learned art historian and –

MARCO: (*makes the sign of the cross, quietly murmuring the Latin*) *In nomine patris, et filii, et spiritus sancti,* amen.

ZEN: – While it is true the cardinal curtsies before the bishop of Rome, I can assure all present that his investigation will be conducted with a most Venetian serenity. This is no Spanish Inquisition. Do I have that correct, Cardinal Archbishop?

BORROMEO: Yes, you do.

ZEN: Discover the painting.

(*The mounted painting is unveiled:* The Brotherhood of the Rosary, *by Albrecht Dürer, circa 1506. It's huge.*)

ZEN: In the month of April in this, the year of our Lord 1606, his Imperial Majesty Rudolf the Second, Holy Roman Emperor, being a great lover and patron of the arts, purchased from the Church of St. Bartolomeo, here in Venice, a painting by one Albrecht Dürer, a northern artist of the last century. *The Brotherhood of the Rosary*. His instructions were for the painting to be swaddled with cloth sealed in wax. And then the four strongest men in Venice should be got – this same honour to be determined in an open competition – to raise the protected painting above their heads and carry it to the imperial residence in Prague, Bohemia, (*pointing*) that way, thus preventing any injury that might be inflicted from its transport in a cart.

A simple task. How I wish it had been completed. How I wish the Venetian army had not been required to retrieve it; how I wish the Captain charged to chaperone had done his job –

CAPTAIN: (*grunts*)

ZEN: How I wish news of a miracle had not leapt from mountaintop to mountaintop, or that the church had not caught wind of it, or that the emperor had not caught wind of it. He's mad, you know. Raving. Spends all his time consulting with astrologers and magicians. But he has been kind enough to allow us to question his errant mercenary and to extend our holding of his canvas, if only because he is keen to establish the veracity of this alleged miracle. I am confident that our prelate is made of sterner stuff and will arrive at the truth.

And so, without further ado, I will ask you all to make your way through that door there, all but (*brief consultation with the Archbishop*) the oarmaker, Marco Chodeschino.

(*Everyone clears the room with the exception of Borromeo, Zen and Marco. Rafal lingers for a moment, his hand on Marco's shoulder. When he releases, Marco makes the sign of the cross.*)

ACT ONE, SCENE TWO

(*Borromeo interviews Marco.*)

BORROMEO: Do you know why we're here, Marco?

MARCO: You want me to tell you what happened, on my, in my, on *our* travel.

BORROMEO: You carried the painting –

MARCO: With the others –

BORROMEO: Over the Alps.

MARCO: Halfway to Prague.

BORROMEO: To the town of –

MARCO: Pusterwald.

BORROMEO: Pusterwald, yes. And something happened there.

MARCO: You want me to tell you about that.

BORROMEO: In time. We should go in order.

MARCO: From the beginning.

BORROMEO: Yes.

ZEN: And try not to be intimidated by the archbishop, Marco. Remember, you are a Venetian.

MARCO: (*his hand is moving to his forehead*) Yes sir.

ZEN: A secular state, the pope our natural enemy.

MARCO: (*sign of the cross*) Sir.

ZEN: You need not look at me like that, Signore.

MARCO: Oh no, I –

ZEN: He started it, not us. Wars of expansion, excommunication; the last thing we need is a miracle on our hands, so close to this, our *Serenissima* –

BORROMEO: Councillor –

ZEN: I'm merely putting the oarmaker at his ease, Eminence.

MARCO: Maybe someone else should go first; someone more at ease.

BORROMEO: Don't be afraid, Marco. The councillor will not speak anymore. And I think you will give me a straightforward story. Then I will use the others to add *colorito* and *disegno*.

MARCO: But I cannot tell a story. I'm not clever like that.

BORROMEO: Clever never helps, my child.

MARCO: Could help me, time from time.

BORROMEO: Marco, there was a famous painter, last century, very highly regarded, very clever. He once painted a scene with many saints crowded around the Virgin and child.

MARCO: Like this one.

BORROMEO: Yes, exactly. But not this one.

MARCO: Not this one.

BORROMEO: Not this one. A different one.

MARCO: Oh.

BORROMEO: One of the saints in this other nativity, not this one, was Christopher. Do you know St. Christopher?

MARCO: Who carried Baby Jesus across a river.

BORROMEO: Precisely. And because the painter wanted you to recognize Christopher, he depicted him in this other nativity –

not this one – holding our blessed saviour on his shoulder, just as we know him. Do you see the problem?

MARCO: (*after a moment's thought*) Baby Jesus was two times in the painting.

BORROMEO: A nativity with two saviours. That's where cleverness can get you if you're not careful.

MARCO: There you go.

BORROMEO: Simple, Marco.

MARCO: Simple.

BORROMEO: From the beginning.

MARCO: I won the strongman prize by lifting a donkey, judges called three names then mine, fourth place, third place, second place, then mine, when they called my name I ran down to claim my prize, but they didn't give me a prize, they gave me a task, and they were already arguing about the boy, Rafal, whether he should be part of the task, they thought he should not do it, I said I would help him –

BORROMEO: Wait.

MARCO: Sorry?

BORROMEO: Simple is not necessarily swift.

MARCO: Oh. I'll start again –

BORROMEO: No. You ensured that young Rafal would stay in the expedition. Why?

MARCO: He wanted to stay. He said he could do it.

BORROMEO: What was that to you?

MARCO: He was fourth place, fair and square!

BORROMEO: So you only helped him to be fair?

MARCO: He lifted a cart full of cabbages with one hand!

BORROMEO: Really.

MARCO: When the judges asked him how he did it, he said he imagined it was St. Mark beneath.

BORROMEO: Beneath what?

MARCO: The cabbages.

BORROMEO: I don't understand.

MARCO: St. Mark beneath the cabbages?

BORROMEO: I don't recall a story of the evangelist Mark hiding under cabbages.

MARCO: No, ha! No.

ZEN: No, no.

MARCO: Ha! No.

ZEN: Ha!

MARCO: Not the man. His bones. It's a story for us. For Venetians. From long time past. How we stole his bones from under the Musselmen's noses and brought them home to Venice.

BORROMEO: And young Rafal said he was able to lift the cart –

MARCO: By imagining those same bones under the cabbages!

BORROMEO: You saw him do it?

MARCO: Made me forget I was missing dinner with my wife and *bambini*.

BORROMEO: You have *bambini*.

MARCO: My joy! – Your Eminence. Two boys and a girl.

BORROMEO: Must have hurt to leave them.

MARCO: The expedition was long, yes. *Gloria della Serenissima.*

BORROMEO: To carry a heavy painting.

MARCO: Heavier and heavier.

BORROMEO: And the Captain was –

(*The Captain appears, unfettered, cleaned up, as if marching.*)

MARCO: Cruel man.

BORROMEO: You must have regretted helping the boy stay on. To let such a frail creature endure these hardships.

(*The others appear, each at their corner of the crate. Marco takes his corner.*)

MARCO: Rafal wanted to go! Said it again and again. And he never once complain.

COCCO: Heavy! Urgh!

MARCO: It were always Cocco who complained. And he was a strongman. So –

COCCO: Who will lighten my mood!

MARCO: You'd think a soldier would not talk like that.

COCCO: Truth is, I been starting to get a bit sick at the sight of blood. Too much killing. I thought this caprice might lead to something better. Urgh! Always such rotten luck! Oh, what am I to do with this useless, excremental life?

BORROMEO: He said all that?

MARCO: He did all the complaining. All of it.

BORROMEO: But I mean, he had no stammer?

MARCO: Oh. Benasuto Cocco only stammer in front of men like you. Among men like me, he speak very well.

BORROMEO: Go on.

MARCO: So then the Captain says –

CAPTAIN: You want to get away from the sight of blood? Then you never should have signed up for this expedition.

COCCO: Why is that?

MARCO: – Cocco ask.

CAPTAIN: Oh, you'll find out soon enough.

MARCO: – says the Captain.

(*Scene. They are holding the painting in a crate above their heads, Marco and Rafal in front, Cocco and Dolfin behind, somewhere in the Alps, having been halted by the Captain.*)

CAPTAIN: Nothing but papist-hating Protestants all the way from here to the emperor's front door.

DOLFIN: We're not papists.

CAPTAIN: You look like papists.

DOLFIN: We do?

CAPTAIN: But you can leave the painting with me and scatter on home. No one will ever know.

DOLFIN: How will you carry it?

CAPTAIN: I have friends. Protestant friends.

DOLFIN: I don't see any friends.

CAPTAIN: They're waiting in Pusterwald. I'll send for them. They'll carry. You'll get paid.

DOLFIN: Okay.

MARCO: You mean I can go home?

DOLFIN: *Fortuna bella*, we can go home!

RAFAL: I'm not afraid to look like a papist. And I shall carry this painting by myself to Prague if I have to.

DOLFIN: Oh.

RAFAL: But do what you must.

MARCO: If he will carry, then so will I.

DOLFIN: Oh.

CAPTAIN: Put your faith in a stupid boy. Typical folly of the papist.

MARCO: What do you mean?

CAPTAIN: Always believing the wrong person will save him. When last the white smoke was released for the new pope, and the bells of St. Peter's began to ring, do you know what the people heard from deep in the bowels of a Roman prison?

MARCO: No.

CAPTAIN: A voice that cried, 'Now I will be free, for he buggered me when I was a boy!'

(*Zen laughs. Borromeo shoots him a concerned look. Marco makes the sign of the cross. The Captain laughs.*)

BORROMEO: Councillor, please!

CAPTAIN: Tell me, boy. How many times have you received such unwanted attention from your pale priests?

RAFAL: But who says I did not want it?

CAPTAIN: I think you misunderstand me.

RAFAL: What? I'm sure I don't. I'll bet you've had more men than I, what with your custom tailoring.

CAPTAIN: Are you implying that I – ?

RAFAL: Hardly an implication.

(*The Captain backhands the boy across his head. Rafal falls to the ground. Marco lets go of his corner and lunges at the Captain, who drops his lance, draws a dagger and holds it at Marco's throat, stopping him.*)

CAPTAIN: Lay one finger on me, strongman, and you shall find yourself bereft of a throat for bleating.

RAFAL: It's all right, Marco. The boy-lover's blow was not so strong.

CAPTAIN: Oh, you want love?

COCCO: Easy, Captain. Don't you need all four to do this job?

CAPTAIN: Get up then, boy. Pick up your cross!

RAFAL: (*still down, as if it's very sweet*) You're comparing me to Jesus.

CAPTAIN: Come on. You can't be that hurt.

(*He prods the boy with his long lance. Marco grabs the lance.*)

MARCO: Leave him alone!

(*The two struggle with it for a moment, before Marco pushes the lance away, knocking the Captain back a few steps and returning to tend to the boy. The Captain sets his lance to attack and looks like he's about to run Marco through.*)

RAFAL: I can do it. (*getting up*) I can do it.

CAPTAIN: So we are ready to resume this sorry expedition?

RAFAL: Yes sir.

CAPTAIN: March!

(*They resume.*)

RAFAL: After all, I am the fourth strongest man in Venice.

MARCO: He did things like that. After a terrible thing, he would say something clever like that. He was strong. Not beaten down. Not like me. Clever. That first night, he tell me about the place we were walking to.

(*Scene. The group of four are settled around a campfire. The Captain is sleeping some distance away by another fire, sword and lance at the ready. Marco engages the boy in conversation. Rafal has a black eye.*)

RAFAL: The mountains will be long gone by then, you know.

MARCO: Truly? They don't go forever?

RAFAL: They don't.

MARCO: I've heard Prague is more beautiful even than Venice.

RAFAL: I've been there.

DOLFIN: You have?

RAFAL: One might say I was born there.

ZEN: (*to Borromeo*) One might say?

MARCO: Born there?

ZEN: (*to Borromeo*) Was he born there or not?

DOLFIN: So that's where you're from.

MARCO: Tell us about Prague, Rafal.

RAFAL: Prague. (*sighs*) Seven hills. A winding river. Winding streets. A city like the world made small. And the castle like the city made small. And the emperor: he too is small.

MARCO: Is he as mad as they say?

RAFAL: He is not so mad. Sweet, you know. Shy. Not mad. He doesn't know what to believe and so he believes everything. And he protects the wandering people in that city. What are they called?

DOLFIN: You mean the Jews?

RAFAL: Yes. Even them. Even the Jews.

ZEN: He did not know how to call the Jews?

RAFAL: He collects alchemists too. Were you not employed by an alchemist, Dolfin?

DOLFIN: A man has to eat.

RAFAL: But the emperor is fascinated by them.

DOLFIN: Really?

RAFAL: Really.

DOLFIN: Are you saying – ?

RAFAL: Not all alchemists are charlatans, Dolfin. He will introduce you to the best in the world.

DOLFIN: He will?

RAFAL: And you're equipped to assist them. You're going to be rich, Dolfin.

DOLFIN: No –

RAFAL: You're going to be rich!

DOLFIN: I believe you. Even if you're lying, it doesn't matter. I'm going to be rich!

MARCO: What else does the emperor like?

RAFAL: I know he peers through telescopes at the stars. Spying on them.

DOLFIN: (*to himself, settling back*) I'm going to be rich!

RAFAL: Though in truth the stars do not like to be spied on so.

MARCO: You talk about the stars like they're in their skivvies.

RAFAL: They are in their skivvies.

COCCO: Maybe they're in their skivvies because they're trying to SLEEP.

DOLFIN: Cocco. We know your bark is worse than your bite.

COCCO: He likes art too, that mad emperor of yours.

RAFAL: How do you know that?

COCCO: Kid. Ask my sore legs how I know. My hips. My back.

RAFAL: Clever Cocco. We carry the emperor's love of art on our backs.

BORROMEO: You became friends.

MARCO: All of us. That Captain mash us together like olive juice and *aglio*.

BORROMEO: And then?

MARCO: And then we came to Pusterwald.

ZEN: That's all?

MARCO: You want more? Let me think. (*He closes his eyes.*)

BORROMEO: What are you doing, Marco?

MARCO: I try to remember the trees, the animals, how cold it got when the sun went down.

ZEN: So you came to Pusterwald.

MARCO: We came to Pusterwald.

BORROMEO: Which was off your path.

MARCO: Was it?

BORROMEO: Two hours off your path.

MARCO: Oh.

BORROMEO: And you were taken.

MARCO: By the Protestants, yes.

BORROMEO: The iconoclasts.

MARCO: That means –

BORROMEO: Men who seek to throw paintings on the fire.

MARCO: Those were them, yes. Those – iconoclaves.

BORROMEO: Iconoclasts.

MARCO: Iconoclasts.

BORROMEO: Do you think the Captain set that up?

MARCO: I think he did. I know he did. He were an iconoclave too.

BORROMEO: What happened?

MARCO: We were going along. Through some passes. But now we had crossed a river. In a valley. We heard a man shout. Something like, 'To the church!' It was ahead of us so we tried to hide.

BORROMEO: Who gave you the order to hide?

MARCO: What do you mean?

BORROMEO: Did someone tell you to conceal yourselves?

MARCO: I think we just did it. No. Maybe it was …

BORROMEO: Yes?

MARCO: Maybe …

> (*The scene is fully engaged, with the four men carrying the crate about their heads. They're in a panic, though, trying to move in all directions, making their task comically precarious.*)

COCCO: What was that?

DOLFIN: Scare me shitless.

MARCO: Look at all those people.

CAPTAIN: It's a church. They're fighting over a church. Get down!

> (*They manage to manoeuvre themselves to a place of safety, using their burden as a shield to hide behind. They set it up like a sort of lean-to that they can peek around and over to observe the action, which takes place offstage for the most part. Cocco pokes his head out to look at what's happening.*)

DOLFIN: What do you see?

COCCO: Oh!

DOLFIN: What?

COCCO: I can see the church. It's just up the road. Modest little thing.

DOLFIN: The fighting, Cocco. What's happening with the fighting?

COCCO: So far mostly like one of our fist wars.

MARCO: You love the fist wars?

COCCO: I do love the fist wars.

MARCO: I'm a player in that.

DOLFIN: Of course you are.

MARCO: (*weakly*) *Guerra dei pugni!*

COCCO: Oh! (*He sits back down beneath the shelter.*)

DOLFIN: What are you doing?

COCCO: It just got bad.

CAPTAIN: It will get a lot worse if it drifts this way.

MARCO: *Fortuna.*

COCCO: (*to Dolfin*) Can't you make us invisible or something?

DOLFIN: Me?

COCCO: Kid said you were an alchemist or –

DOLFIN: Magic isn't real, my friend. (*Cocco laughs.*) Oh you're just making fun of me, aren't you, ha ha ha. (*He switches places with Cocco and looks out.*)
Look at that: They're taking spades to each other.

MARCO: (*makes the sign of the cross*) Thank you, Lord, for protecting our frail bodies with your likeness.

RAFAL: (*imitates the sign of the cross*) Should we not be hiding the painting?

MARCO: The painting is hiding us.

DOLFIN: The Catholics are retreating.

CAPTAIN: There it is.

COCCO: How do you know it's the Catholics?

DOLFIN: There's a priest! Oh! Ow!

COCCO: What now?

DOLFIN: Someone threw a stone, it hit him in the head!

MARCO: The priest?

DOLFIN: Now they're pulling him away.

MARCO: Mary and Joseph.

DOLFIN: The Protestants are letting them go!

CAPTAIN: No killing a priest today.

DOLFIN: What do we do now?

CAPTAIN: Wait for that rabble to go home.

COCCO: Oh bugger.

DOLFIN: Now what?

COCCO: They're coming this way.

CAPTAIN: They're not.

COCCO: They are.

CAPTAIN: You speak with them.

COCCO: Sorry?

CAPTAIN: Better I am not seen. You speak with them. I'll come later. (*He withdraws.*)

COCCO: But ... Captain ...

RAFAL: Captain –

DOLFIN: Where is he going? Shouldn't he be – ? (*pointing to the approaching crowd*)

COCCO: I didn't think a man like that could run.

ZEN: So your Cap–

    COCCO: (*calling after the Captain*) I thought the pike up his ass would slow him down!

ZEN: So your Captain abandoned you.

MARCO: He came later with his three fellows.

BORROMEO: What fellows?

MARCO: Those Landser fellows. Lanseks– Lans ... kecks.

BORROMEO: Landsknechts.

MARCO: *Già*, them.

BORROMEO: And what happened to you?

MARCO: Well, first the mob took us. They said we were a papal procession of monks! We told them we were not.

BORROMEO: And they didn't believe you.

MARCO: They took us into that church as prisoners.

BORROMEO: The one they were fighting over.

MARCO: They tied us up, locked us inside. It was funny, though: they were afraid of our crate.

BORROMEO: Why is that funny?

MARCO: It wasn't funny.

BORROMEO: You just said it was funny.

MARCO: Is that wrong?

BORROMEO: No, Marco. I just want to know why they were afraid of the crate.

MARCO: They think: if four men wear black, they must be monks, if monks are carrying a crate, there must be something hidden in the crate; if it's hidden it must be bad, if it's bad it's the devil. So the devil is in the crate. Crazy. So then they want to burn it. But they were curious. So they want to see it first. But they were afraid to open it, to see it, to burn it. Funny. Better if they had not feared it. If they had not feared it, they could have burned it straight.

BORROMEO: Curiosity and fear go hand in hand.

MARCO: Ha. Ya. But it was good to see how they were scared of something I was not scared of.

BORROMEO: That must have helped.

MARCO: They left us for an hour. Then they came back. And the Captain was with them.

BORROMEO: Your Captain.

MARCO: There he was. Our Captain! With three other Lands–

BORROMEO: –knechts.

MARCO: *Già*, like himself.

BORROMEO: Were they the friends he'd spoken of?

MARCO: I don't know. But he pretend he did not know us.

COCCO: I was in the Battle of Lepanto!

MARCO: Oh yeah. And then Cocco tried to save us. With all his words.

COCCO: I'm a veteran!

BORROMEO: Cocco?

MARCO: Tried to make them remember how we all hate the Turk.

COCCO: Marco was in the battle too!

MARCO: What?

COCCO: Give us some credit!

MARCO: He say I was in the battle too. Then, he say something about a sick man, mothers, slicing enemies, clenching hearts, wiser men, the Turk, gods –

COCCO: Men can be better! Don't leave it to chance! Don't waste time on gods! It brings no good to anyone for men to destroy the works of other men.

BORROMEO: It did not work.

MARCO: When he finish, Rafal spoke up.

RAFAL: Your words won't help you, Cocco. I can do better.

BORROMEO: He made a better argument?

MARCO: He made a miracle.

BORROMEO: And you remember?

MARCO: I remember all of it.

(*To the scene. The hands of all the men are bound behind their backs.*)

RAFAL: They're saying the devil is right here in this crate, Cocco. What's the Turk to that?

COCCO: Shut up, kid.

RAFAL: (*still to Cocco, but including the people*) You're trying so hard to make these people change the way they feel in their hearts. That cunning kind of talk was *invented* by the devil! You devil-talker, you, Cocco!

COCCO: Kid!

RAFAL: But he loves eloquence, the devil. He would banish all the gods to hear one fine human thought. (*He sneezes into the neck of his jersey, turning to the people.*) You people, if you don't believe me, you should knock on the wood and ask him yourself!

(*Marco gasps, caught up in the story.*)

BORROMEO: He was telling them the devil was in the box?

RAFAL: Imagine being in the dark like that, lonely as the stars, just wanting to come out and talk to people!

MARCO: He made them think, more and more, there was a devil in the box. And instead of wanting to see it less, they want to see it more!

RAFAL: I'd like to see that. Wouldn't you? You want to see that, don't you. Open it!

MARCO: And so they did.

BORROMEO: And they saw the painting.

MARCO: Yes. There was a hush. But then someone shout how it has a pope there and a priest there, so it is a papist painting and should be burnt.

RAFAL: It is the Virgin Mother.

MARCO: They all step back to look at it, hatred in their eyes. The Captain was there too. Hatred in his eyes. He step forward and said something in the German language.

CAPTAIN: *Landsknechte! Vortreten!*

BORROMEO: What did he say?

MARCO: I think he told them to burn it. But then, before they have a chance, Rafal say:

RAFAL: Look everyone; look at the painting. (*with a gesture*) Mother.

MARCO: And then out steps the Virgin Mary. The real Virgin Mary. Holding the baby.

DOLFIN: Brilliant.

COCCO: I'll be buggered.

CAPTAIN: I have gone mad!

MARCO: The Virgin Mother smiles. Bares her breast puts the infant to it.

CAPTAIN: Forgive me I am weak!

MARCO: He fell to his knees so did I.

CAPTAIN: I am weak.

MARCO: Then the Virgin Mother step back into the painting, just like that, and came back just like she is now.

BORROMEO: Same as before.

DOLFIN: Brilliant.

MARCO: Same but different to us. All of us.

BORROMEO: Some say the Virgin took a broom and swept the church.

ZEN: Oh, Archbishop, don't encourage him.

MARCO: No, she did not clean.

BORROMEO: You're sure?

MARCO: I would have remembered.

ZEN: He would have remembered, Archbishop.

BORROMEO: Excuse me, Councillor, but –

ZEN: (*to Marco*) And how did the painting look when she had stepped out of it?

MARCO: Sorry?

ZEN: Were the Virgin and child absent from the painting when they had stepped out from it?

MARCO: Well ... like His Eminence said, a person can't be two places at once.

ZEN: But I'm asking specifically: did you see the empty place in the painting?

MARCO: I –

ZEN: Was the angel still there, for example?

MARCO: Angel?

ZEN: (*indicating the figure in the painting*) There. With the lute. Did she have to step around the angel to come out of the painting?

BORROMEO: Councillor –

ZEN: Did she tread upon the pope's exquisite robe?

MARCO: I did not see.

ZEN: No.

BORROMEO: A word, Councillor. (*They withdraw.*) I wonder if it isn't counter to the spirit of this inquiry to have you participate.

ZEN: Oh?

BORROMEO: You promised these men it would not be an inquisition.

ZEN: Harmless questions.

BORROMEO: From the magistrate of the *Serenissima*.

ZEN: Would you have even thought to ask these questions?

BORROMEO: If I thought they were relevant.

ZEN: They are relevant.

BORROMEO: For me to decide.

ZEN: Very well. I can be silent as well as I can speak.

BORROMEO: I was hoping for something a little more categorical.

ZEN: What, leave the room? ...
Very well, Archbishop. I yield the floor entire.

(*Exit Zen.*)

MARCO: Where is he going?

BORROMEO: Don't worry, Marco.

MARCO: I'm not worried.

RAFAL: (*he has been untied*) My friends, please listen, understand, this painting is heading to the Emperor Rudolf in the city of Prague. Venetians do not like to be tardy with their transactions.

MARCO: But it was not so easy anymore. Now a miracle had taken place. The people wanted to keep it for themselves. They all just turned their colours in a moment.

BORROMEO: Roman Catholic.

MARCO: Just like that. It took the Venetian troops to come and take the painting off their hands. Bring it back here where we will have to start all over again to get to Prague.

BORROMEO: And the other mercenary soldiers, they became Catholics too?

MARCO: So I was told.

BORROMEO: But not your own guard.

MARCO: Proud man. Evil.

BORROMEO: You think he brought you to that town on purpose.

MARCO: You say that as if there were some doubt.

BORROMEO: Is there any doubt?

MARCO: I have no doubt.

BORROMEO: That's an answer.

MARCO: Why Venice hire a man like that in the first place?

BORROMEO: Not Venice, Marco. The Landsknecht mercenary army is in the employ of the emperor. They're considered the best soldiers in the world, that's why the emperor wanted him to be your guard.

MARCO: What will happen to him?

BORROMEO: That is not for me to say. He's been tried and condemned.

MARCO: How did they call his crime?

BORROMEO: Conspiracy to theft and destruction.

MARCO: So it's clear.

BORROMEO: As things of this world can be.

MARCO: It's a funny thing.

BORROMEO: What is?

MARCO: I guess he really did hate that painting because of the pope on there, and that priest ... (*He's staring at the painting.*) Because they weren't there, at Baby Jesus's birth ...

BORROMEO: Yes?

MARCO: No, it's wrong. They're not my beliefs, just my thoughts. But I want to tell them you. But they're wrong, but I want to tell you and not make it a sin!

BORROMEO: You wish to make a confession?

MARCO: Bless me, Father, for I have sinned. It is two months since my last confession.

BORROMEO: Why so long?

MARCO: Your Eminence, we was in the Alps.

BORROMEO: Of course. So.

MARCO: I think I might be an – iconoclave.

BORROMEO: Iconoclast.

MARCO: I think that might be me.

BORROMEO: Why?

MARCO: There is one thing in my own church here in Venice that I would destroy.

BORROMEO: Let's hear it.

MARCO: I would … it's wrong but I would … I go inside, see? To pray? And I see the priest making the sacrament. All the poor people around, like me.

BORROMEO: Yes? My child?

MARCO: What I don't like is when he have a rich man who want to give him money. There's a word for that too.

BORROMEO: Patron.

MARCO: Give money to the church. Good, yes? You think that would be enough. But no: the man, rich man, want his family crest on the robes of the priest. Right there on the chest of the priest. And the priest allow it. He wear that family crest while blessing the sacrament like he were no more than a sign hanging out in front of an apothecary.

BORROMEO: This is what you took away from witnessing a miracle?

MARCO: I think I would like to tear that crest off his robe; that's what I think now; that priest don't even know the difference between right and wrong. I mean, has he ever seen a miracle? I don't think so.

BORROMEO: Marco, are you calling yourself better than a priest ordained by God?

MARCO: I ... no ...

BORROMEO: Are you sure?

MARCO: Well, maybe that one. I'm sorry, but when you've seen a miracle, like I have, a real miracle –

BORROMEO: That's a grave sin, Marco.

MARCO: Is it?

BORROMEO: Your penance must be severe.

MARCO: Name it!

BORROMEO: Are you truly sorry?

MARCO: I am!

BORROMEO: Three sets of fifty Ave Marias, my child.

(*Marco looks up.*)

BORROMEO: And I would have you hand over one of your boys for a lifetime's service to the church.

MARCO: One of my –

BORROMEO: Take him to the door of the Santa Maria del Rosario tomorrow morning and present him to the *Jesuati* there.

MARCO: Please, Your Eminence. My younger, he is so young.

BORROMEO: Then choose your older boy.

MARCO: But he is my eldest.

BORROMEO: Console yourself, my child, that one day you will understand how the lifelong sacrifice to the church is a world away from witnessing miracles. (*sign of the cross*) *In nomine patris, et filii, et spiritus sancti,* amen.

ACT ONE, SCENE THREE

(*Borromeo and the Captain. The Captain is still cruelly fettered.*)

CAPTAIN: You're going to provoke me.

BORROMEO: No ...

CAPTAIN: You're going to say something like, 'Martin Luther was born from the union of the devil and a nun.'

BORROMEO: I will not express such an opinion.

CAPTAIN: But you believe it.

BORROMEO: What I believe is of no consequence in this investigation. I'm trying to determine what you believe. Or, more specifically, what took place.

CAPTAIN: Good luck with that.

BORROMEO: Did you witness the boy's some say miraculous inclusion among the four strongest men in Venice?

CAPTAIN: It hardly matters what he did. It was still insanity to include him. He was weak and made my task so much harder.

BORROMEO: Unless your task was to destroy the painting.
You have no answer to that?

CAPTAIN: I would shrug, but the iron prevents me.

BORROMEO: You do not deny it?

CAPTAIN: I denied it three times. Each time a hot coal was pressed into my liver. Your Councillor Zen –

BORROMEO: – is no longer here. There are no torturers present.

CAPTAIN: Oh, have we left Venice? Are we in Utopia? Am I dead?

BORROMEO: You will not trust me.

CAPTAIN: If you let me out of these fetters, I will speak the truth of what I saw and what I believed to the best of my knowledge. If I stay like this, I can only gibber and cry like a dog.

BORROMEO: Very well.

(*A guard comes and releases the Captain. He falls to the ground. Struggles to rise.*)

BORROMEO: Take your time.

CAPTAIN: (*weeping, trying to hide it*) Thank you. (*He finds his feet.*) Though, I must confess this confinement has rendered my mind a weakened tool.

BORROMEO: Bring the Captain some water.

CAPTAIN: My task was twofold. One, to ensure that the painting came to Prague safely, and two, to ensure the safety of those four who carried it. Everything I did was with these directives in mind. One and two.

BORROMEO: But you tried to take the painting from them.

CAPTAIN: Indeed. That was in the interest of Directive Two with a logical extension that it was also in the interest of Directive One.

BORROMEO: I find that hard to believe.

CAPTAIN: March!

(*With a great effort, the Captain raises his enfeebled arms to make a gesture that starts the scene. Perhaps he needs to do it twice: first for the front pair, then for the back. The four are trudging through with their cargo. The Captain hesitates, turning back to Borromeo.*)

CAPTAIN: I require my weapons.

BORROMEO: Surely you can tell your story without them.

CAPTAIN: Not with any authority ... Look at me, Bishop. Look at me.

BORROMEO: Very well. Who am I to stand in the way of verisimilitude? (*to the guards*) Watch him.

(*The Captain is handed his weapons: a pike, a sword and, after some hesitation on the part of the guard, a dagger, whereupon he takes up the rear with the energy of the past. Slow progress.*)

CAPTAIN: I have been given the impossible task of protecting four dead men.

MARCO: (*sign of the cross with the mumbled words*)

CAPTAIN: Don't do that.

MARCO: Why not?

CAPTAIN: Not that it matters. As if your proclivities aren't obvious for miles around.

DOLFIN: What's obvious for – ?

COCCO: Why are you calling us four dead men?

CAPTAIN: It's nothing personal. Since I've been assigned to protect you then it follows I'm a dead man too.
(*Pause. They're all looking back at him.*)
Halt!
(*They halt.*)
Well, look at yourselves.
The way you're dressed. The cargo you carry. You look like a papist procession of a holy relic.

DOLFIN: We do?

COCCO: No we don't.

CAPTAIN: Yes you do.

DOLFIN: We look like a – ?

COCCO: No, we don't. How could we, we're –

CAPTAIN: Marching into quiet lands where everyone goes about his quiet routine as though he would not murder any papist who might happen across his path.

MARCO: (*sign of the cross*)

CAPTAIN: Stop that. These lands are full of Protestants, living under the empire's ineffectual, nominally Catholic king. It's only a matter of time before they touch a match to the powder keg.

DOLFIN: But we're not papists.

MARCO: I am.

DOLFIN: If you're a Venetian, you're not a papist.

CAPTAIN: So I thought.

MARCO: How can you say that?

DOLFIN: The whole city was excommunicated by the pope –

MARCO: Oh that.

DOLFIN: Less than a month ago.

MARCO: That's got nothing to do with me.

DOLFIN: But it does!

CAPTAIN: The point is not that you are papists.

DOLFIN: You're a Venetian, my friend.

MARCO: I am but –

DOLFIN: No buts!

CAPTAIN: The point is you *look* like papists.

MARCO: I *am* a papist.

DOLFIN: Shut up.

RAFAL: I'm a papist too!

MARCO: The boy's a papist too! (*laughs*) No matter what you think! Two papists so you can all shut up!

DOLFIN: *Cretino*, can't you hear what the man's saying?

MARCO: Who you calling *cretino*?

DOLFIN: He's saying it's dangerous to talk like that in the mountains.

CAPTAIN: And more dangerous to look the way you do. You look like papist priests.

DOLFIN: We do not.

CAPTAIN: You do.

MARCO: What, the black? Can it be so bad?

CAPTAIN: I was once called in to restore order at a funeral march in Dresden. Papist. A zealous Protestant mob had cracked open the casket and ripped the corpse to pieces.

DOLFIN: (*indicating part of his garment*) But this part isn't black, it's not black this part, that's not papist, that's not monkish, I didn't know we looked monkish, monkish clothes don't fit, they're not tailored, this is tailored, but we should get out of these clothes, right? So what if we don't have any other clothes? I don't have any other clothes still we should get out of these clothes we should go naked.

CAPTAIN: Naked but still bearing a holy relic.

DOLFIN: This painting is a holy relic?

MARCO: (*sign of the cross*)

CAPTAIN: Don't do that. The Bible says, 'Thou shalt not make unto thee any graven image.'

MARCO: How can that be the Bible? I understand it.

CAPTAIN: Because it's been translated.

COCCO: Anyone tries to cross us, we'll explain. We'll tell them we're labourers.

CAPTAIN: You'll explain.

COCCO: Venetian labourers, excommunicants. Venetians wear black.

CAPTAIN: You're a soldier, right?

COCCO: I was.

CAPTAIN: Yet you think there'll be time for words.

COCCO: Then give us weapons.

CAPTAIN: I'm not going to do that.

COCCO: You're not.

CAPTAIN: I have the impression none of you care for me.

COCCO: So what do you suggest, Captain? Or did you bring it all up just to scare us?

CAPTAIN: I have an idea that will benefit everyone.

COCCO: What is it?

CAPTAIN: I have confederates. Three of them. Landsknechts who will carry this painting with me. Such men will not draw attention in these mountains.

DOLFIN: You're saying –

CAPTAIN: I'm saying we can correct this fool's errand. I propose that we lay low, right here, tonight. I send for my friends, they come here and we send the four of you on a luxurious wagon ride through all the passes of the mountains and beyond, to disembark just south of Prague.

MARCO: A wagon ride.

CAPTAIN: A luxurious wagon ride.

DOLFIN: We go from certain death to a luxurious wagon ride.

COCCO: And then what happens?

CAPTAIN: Then you rendezvous with our party, take up your burden again, and finally enter the city in triumph, no one the wiser.

MARCO: Triumph?

DOLFIN: That seems so easy.

MARCO: But we'd be liars.

CAPTAIN: Is it not worth a little lie, strongman, to return safe to your family?

MARCO: I –

COCCO: And you will be protected too.

CAPTAIN: Indeed.

COCCO: Fulfilling both your directives.

CAPTAIN: I am nothing if not a tactician.

DOLFIN: It's –

CAPTAIN: – safe passage through the mountains for all of us.

DOLFIN: Do we still get our ducats?

CAPTAIN: And more: the chance to visit a great city, burden-free.

MARCO: It's a good deal.

CAPTAIN: Especially for a true-blue papist like you.

MARCO: (*sign of the cross*)

CAPTAIN: Please.

MARCO: Sorry. (*He does it again.*)

CAPTAIN: What do the others think?

DOLFIN: I think it's a miracle.

COCCO: I think this man is too quick to join the crowd.

CAPTAIN: And you?

COCCO: I think there's a snare.

CAPTAIN: No snare.

COCCO: Oh, well, since there's no snare –

CAPTAIN: I invite you to think of one.

COCCO: I'm trying. I can't. Except –

CAPTAIN: What?

COCCO: – what if somebody reported us?

CAPTAIN: To the emperor? That's my job.

COCCO: And Venice?

CAPTAIN: Venice prefers substance over semblance. As long as
the task is done, your Venice will not care who carried.

RAFAL: No.

COCCO: Kid?

RAFAL: No. No. The emperor said the four strongest men from Venice should carry it.

CAPTAIN: Oh, and you're one of those.

RAFAL: I am.

CAPTAIN: I'm giving you a chance for safe passage –

RAFAL: Which is your job, it seems to me. Not ours.

CAPTAIN: Everyone here is against you.

MARCO: Not me.

DOLFIN: Oh, I was really starting to think we were going to do this.

RAFAL: I don't think the Captain has the best interests of the painting at heart.

CAPTAIN: You think I'm not a man of my word?

RAFAL: You'd have us break our word.

CAPTAIN: I just want to do my job.

RAFAL: So do your job!

CAPTAIN: With your cargo for kindling and nothing left of us but a smoulder of black bones, I will not have done my job.

RAFAL: And how can we do ours if we arrive outside the walls of Prague, and wait, and wait, and wait?

CAPTAIN: You think I would fail in my task?

RAFAL: I think you have some other task.

CAPTAIN: What task?

RAFAL: Who knows? Perhaps you don't like the painting.

CAPTAIN: I have two directives –

RAFAL: I do not give my consent.

CAPTAIN: We could say that one strongman was not so strong and did not make it.

RAFAL: Oh.

MARCO: If the boy doesn't choose then neither do I.

DOLFIN: *A vaffanculo.*

CAPTAIN: How can I convince you?

RAFAL: You can't.

CAPTAIN: Typical folly of the papist. Why would I try to deceive you? Why not just kill you?

RAFAL: Less mess.

CAPTAIN: You prefer to get abused by your priests.

RAFAL: What? I'll bet you've had more men than I, what with your custom tailoring.

CAPTAIN: Are you implying that I – ?

RAFAL: Hardly an implication.

(*The Captain backhands the boy across his head. Rafal falls to the ground. Marco lets go of his corner and lunges at the Captain, who drops his lance, draws a dagger and holds it at Marco's throat, stopping him.*)

BORROMEO: So the boy thwarted your plan.

CAPTAIN: If he had let me have my way, the painting would even now be safely in the castle in Prague. And so would I.

BORROMEO: But you gave them no more trouble? After that?

CAPTAIN: I gave them no more trouble.

BORROMEO: But did you not have friends waiting in Pusterwald? Two hours off your path?

CAPTAIN: It was my intention to give these donkeys another chance to consider my offer.

BORROMEO: Except the village had been taken over by iconoclasts.

CAPTAIN: Unbeknownst to me. It was precisely the kind of trouble I had foretold. Anyway, they were Calvinists. I'm Lutheran.

BORROMEO: How do you know they were Calvinists?

CAPTAIN: Because they were crazy.

BORROMEO: They were converted to Catholicism –

CAPTAIN: More proof.

BORROMEO: – by a miracle.

CAPTAIN: Not a miracle.

BORROMEO: What was it if not a mir–?

CAPTAIN: The devil's work!

BORROMEO: Why do you use such a term?

CAPTAIN: Because that's what it was! Because it came from the boy, and the boy did not have any interest in the greater glory of God. Merely to thwart me!

BORROMEO: It came from the boy? To thwart you?

CAPTAIN: With that venomous pleasure of the weaker man who takes down the stronger. He knew I would succeed in putting the painting back on the road. The matter was well in hand.

BORROMEO: How?

CAPTAIN: You don't care. You only care about your miracle.

BORROMEO: How? You abandoned the party when they were captured, and then?

CAPTAIN: You won't believe me.

BORROMEO: Try me.

CAPTAIN: With my confederates, my three *able* confederates, I would have *impressed* upon those ... ignorant people –

BORROMEO: You mean the townspeople –

CAPTAIN: Yes – that we were about the emperor's business, with the cargo, and none of theirs!

BORROMEO: Your confederates were present.

CAPTAIN: Of course they were present.

BORROMEO: Why have they not testified on your behalf?

CAPTAIN: Because –

BORROMEO: Why?

CAPTAIN: Because they embraced your faith, and I – *renounced* them for it!

BORROMEO: And they abandoned you?

CAPTAIN: Content to see me tortured and condemned.

BORROMEO: Your Lutheran faith is so strong. And yet you expect me to believe –

CAPTAIN: Why would I have rushed back here for help?

BORROMEO: Because your ploy had failed?

CAPTAIN: If my task had been to destroy the painting, I would have destroyed the painting! Since my task was to protect the painting –

BORROMEO: Why would anyone want to destroy this painting?

CAPTAIN: Yes, why should I not speak hypothetically as if I'd sought to destroy the painting?

BORROMEO: I am merely asking –

CAPTAIN: Another trap. I would say –

BORROMEO: No –

CAPTAIN: I would say it was a false idol, 'thou shalt not make unto thee – '

BORROMEO: I am trying to determine how this work –

CAPTAIN: Then you would say I am guilty! But I am not guilty!

BORROMEO: I have a directive too, Captain. And it has nothing to do with your innocence or guilt, I'm afraid.

CAPTAIN: (*almost to himself*) I have already been condemned!

BORROMEO: I know.
    My investigation is about that (*the painting*) and only that.
    I can neither save nor condemn you.
    (*The Captain weeps.*)
    I am sorry.
    I just want to know the Protestant thinking.

CAPTAIN: (*returning to himself*) So you're as ignorant as the rest of them.

BORROMEO: Who?

CAPTAIN: Them!

(*The scene. Night. They have made camp.*)

COCCO: With respect, Captain, if you hate the p-papists so much, why would you not destroy this painting we transport?

53

(The others look to him with surprise.)

CAPTAIN: I hardly need to explain myself to you.

COCCO: It depicts a pope.

CAPTAIN: On his knees.

COCCO: Just one of many lies in the painting, from your point of view.

DOLFIN: How can you say a pretty painting is full of lies?

COCCO: You have to think like an iconoclast.

DOLFIN: Surely –

COCCO: Let's have a look! Captain?

CAPTAIN: What?

COCCO: I require a tool.

(The Captain hands over his dagger.)

BORROMEO: You claim to have given him a weapon?

(Taking on the role of the iconoclast, Cocco goes and unveils the painting.)

CAPTAIN: Who am I to stand in the way of a debate, Bishop?

BORROMEO: *(to the guards, referring to the Captain's other weapons on the ground)* Take those. The Captain has found his authority without them.

(The painting.)

MARCO: So beautiful.

RAFAL: Blessed Virgin Mother. Makes me think of my own.

BORROMEO: You allowed them to unveil the painting.

CAPTAIN: Boy. Your mother was hardly a virgin.

COCCO: All right now –

RAFAL: Say that again.

COCCO: Wait now, I'm just going to –

CAPTAIN: (*taunting Rafal*) Your mother. Was hardly. A –

(*Rafal attacks him, leaping onto his back and raining blows down upon his head.*)

COCCO: Hold up! I'm trying to teach you something!

(*They all have to pull the boy off the Captain.*)

DOLFIN: What are you doing? Are you crazy?

RAFAL: No one insults my mother!

DOLFIN: This man can kill you.

RAFAL: So can you.

DOLFIN: I'm not going to kill you!

RAFAL: (*pointing to the Virgin in the painting*) Imagine calling that woman a whore and you'll know how I feel!

CAPTAIN: (*as the others hold Rafal back*) I don't know what your game is, boy. Perhaps you just like to get the stuffing beat out of you from time to time. But if you ever touch me again, I will slice you open from your navel to your jaw.

RAFAL: Take back what you said about my mother.

CAPTAIN: You must be joking!

(*Rafal spits in his face. The Captain lunges at him. Marco has to let go of the boy and impedes the Captain, just as the Captain clutches at Rafal. For a few moments, everyone is connected and clinging to one another as the scrum circles around and then finally pulls apart.*)

MARCO: Please ... please ...

CAPTAIN: He spit in my face!

RAFAL: I'd do it again.

COCCO: We have an exposed painting here. Exposed. To the elements! Show some respect! All of you! Pay attention!

BORROMEO: He would not back down from the belief that his mother was a virgin?

CAPTAIN: As I said.

BORROMEO: But that is unbelievable. Who did he think he was?

CAPTAIN: Your guess, Bishop, is as good as mine.

COCCO: Now. Who will stand in for the artist? (*pulling Dolfin to his feet*)

DOLFIN: What? No!

COCCO: Oh yes. It was your question: 'How can a pretty painting be full of lies?' Are you not an actor? Just act like an artist.

DOLFIN: I –

COCCO: I was not aware, Master Dürer, that there was a Holy Roman Emperor present at the birth of our precious Lord.

DOLFIN: Oh come on.

RAFAL: No it's true. That's exactly what the bastards would say.

COCCO: There he is. Rudolf's great-grandfather, Maximilian, I think. He was at war with Venice, which might explain why we're all carrying this wretched thing away from Venice, but doesn't explain what he's doing in here!

56

DOLFIN: I –

COCCO: And this man. Some pope. How can there be a pope there?

DOLFIN: You tell me.

COCCO: There can't! It's absurd! That babe in arms has yet to invent the concept! And then there's you.

DOLFIN: Me?

COCCO: Yes, that's you.

DOLFIN: That's not me.

COCCO: Are you not the painter Albrecht Dürer? That's you!

DOLFIN: Oh, I see. You meant ... I see.

COCCO: And then, most terrible of all, the painting depicts an evil man, a torturer who should not be present by any measure.

DOLFIN: A torturer?

COCCO: Named, by the papists, a saint.

CAPTAIN: No it does not.

COCCO: Yes, it does. Who do you think this is? (*pointing to the black-robed priest in the painting*)

CAPTAIN: That's just some priest.

DOLFIN: Isn't it?

COCCO: Oh no. That, my friends, is St. Dominic, present in this painting because he invented the rosary.

CAPTAIN: How then is he a torturer?

COCCO: He founded the Spanish Inquisition.

MARCO: Him?

CAPTAIN: A lie. That's merely some village prie–

COCCO: It's St. Dominic, founder of the Inquisition.

CAPTAIN: I don't believe you.

COCCO: Why do you care?

BORROMEO: Why did you care?

CAPTAIN: I – I'll confess I admire the painting. I could not tolerate such lies.

BORROMEO: You admire the painting?

CAPTAIN: I admire the artist. He made dignified drawings of soldiers just like me. He himself became a Lutheran –

BORROMEO: Long after this painting was painted.

CAPTAIN: Still, it figures wisdom in the man, as I see it.

BORROMEO: But the priest in the painting *is* St. Dominic.

CAPTAIN: *That* priest – founded the Inquisition? Founded it?

BORROMEO: I'm afraid so.

CAPTAIN: I'm such a fool.

COCCO: Your turn now, actor. Defend it.

DOLFIN: But the Captain was doing such an exceptional job.

COCCO: He's lost his enthusiasm. Defend it! The iconoclasts are raising their pikes!

DOLFIN: Well, I, um, I don't know much about it, it's a very uh, colourful canvas (*Marco reacts*): the viewer must allow the colours to penetrate his eye, his *eye*, or, the, *aqua permanens*, even, which is to say these colours in this canvas (*Marco reacts*) are distilled with the celestial waters of his eye, the viewer's eye, my eye, almost as if the canvas (*Marco reacts*) were itself a kind of – philosophical stone, if you like, fixed by nature to – fixed by ... nature – I'm sorry, Marco, did you want to say something?

MARCO: It's not canvas.

DOLFIN: I beg your pardon?

MARCO: It's not canvas. It's poplar wood.

DOLFIN: It's –

MARCO: Poplar wood.

DOLFIN: Not canvas.

MARCO: No.

DOLFIN: Poplar wood.

MARCO: See, in Venice, the painters can often paint their paintings on poplar wood. I happen to know that because ... I don't know why I know that, the wood I work with I guess, maybe, I don't know, so, but –

DOLFIN: You work with wood.

MARCO: Yeah, oars, so, I don't know but –

DOLFIN: So it's –

MARCO: Strange, though, because Venice also makes the best canvas in the world.

DOLFIN: Really. See, I don't see how – that matters.

MARCO: I guess ships and sails are more important than paintings when it comes right down to it.

CAPTAIN: Ha! They take all the canvas!

COCCO: Very true. Ships and sails, commerce and war: more important than paintings.

CAPTAIN: Nice.

COCCO: A universal truth. Nice job, Marco.

MARCO: Thank you.

DOLFIN: Good job, Marco. *Magisterium.*

COCCO: The oarmaker knows his wood and canvas, the alchemist's assistant knows his nonsense words, and we mercenary soldiers, we know about the destructive acts of the iconoclast.

(*The Captain indicates that Cocco should give him back his dagger. He does.*)

CAPTAIN: We do. How did you come to it, soldier?

COCCO: Oh, I spent many months destroying art. I stripped whole churches of their frescos. When the statues doubled as columns or buttresses, the whole church came down.

RAFAL: You did that?

COCCO: The money was very good.

CAPTAIN: And why did you stop?

COCCO: A man can only destroy so much.

CAPTAIN: But surely when you slice a canvas to ribbons, you can see there's nothing to it.

COCCO: I like art.

CAPTAIN: Inconvenient for a soldier.

COCCO: Yes it is.

You still haven't answered my question though, Captain. Why do you, a Protestant, not seek this painting's destruction?

CAPTAIN: I do not seek my punishment.

COCCO: In this land rife with anti-papist sentiment? Who would punish you?

CAPTAIN: Why would you provoke me?

BORROMEO: Why would he provoke you?

CAPTAIN: You'll have to ask him.

BORROMEO: And then Pusterwald.

(*Rafal appears, as if in the church.*)

BORROMEO: Where the villagers prevented you from fulfilling your directive.

CAPTAIN: Both my directives. One and two.
(*to the people in the church*) Step away! We are Landsknechts! We are about the emperor's business and none of yours!

BORROMEO: Why did you wait so long to speak?

CAPTAIN: All right, I enjoyed watching those donkeys squirm; but the time was right to strike.

BORROMEO: And then a miracle.

CAPTAIN: Not a miracle.

(*Rafal sneezes into the neck of his jersey.*)

BORROMEO: You know, it wasn't just Protestants who were converted in that moment. There were four secret Musselmen as well. None of this impresses you?

CAPTAIN: I was there, you know. You weren't.

BORROMEO: You claim it was the devil's work.

CAPTAIN: The devil through that boy.

RAFAL: (*with a gesture*) Mother.

BORROMEO: How could you – ?

CAPTAIN: Here I am, Inquisitor: an innocent man, bound, condemned, unbelieved. Is it not reasonable for me to believe it was the devil's work?

BORROMEO: But I'm told you fell to your knees.

CAPTAIN: Yes.

BORROMEO: Said God should forgive you.

CAPTAIN: Yes.

BORROMEO: Why should God forgive you?
> …
> Because you fell.
> To your knees.
> Because you believed.

CAPTAIN: Yes.

BORROMEO: You believed.

CAPTAIN: I believed.

BORROMEO: You believed! Have you considered perhaps that God did indeed guide that boy's hand?

CAPTAIN: I have.

BORROMEO: You have.

CAPTAIN: Of course I have. And so I would have God guide your hand now.

BORROMEO: How.

CAPTAIN: Set me free.

BORROMEO: I cannot.

CAPTAIN: And take that boy.

BORROMEO: Yes?

CAPTAIN: And kill him, before he corrupts even the thinking of a man as wise as you.

BORROMEO: I have nothing to fear from this boy.

CAPTAIN: Oh, you do. I can see it. You consider everything.

BORROMEO: Like you, I relish a good debate.

CAPTAIN: Yes, but I do not allow the debate to change my mind.

BORROMEO: Then what good is a debate?

CAPTAIN: Same as any battle. Victory. Spoils. I think you are a poor Christian. I think you love the thought of this graven image come to life.

BORROMEO: But this is not a graven image.

CAPTAIN: It is!

BORROMEO: And God will correct any error I might indulge –

CAPTAIN: God does not work that way. Nothing should stand between a sorry Christian and his risen Lord. Not the pagans, nor the art that you love, neither ancient nor modern, nor the pale priests of your dying church. Our ways are much simpler than yours. So more clearly will we see the truth. The Protestant path is the rational path, the scientific path, the path to true enlightenment. And all who say, and see, and do, falsehood, like that boy, should have their throats slit.

BORROMEO: That's madness.

CAPTAIN: A madness to which I aspire.

(The Captain holds up the dagger which he has managed to keep, playfully. Then, with a swift move, as the guard lunges, he moves to slit his own throat. Blackout. End of Act One.)

(*Night. In camp. They are by the fire. Cocco is sleeping. The Captain is a little further away, also sleeping. Rafal's eye is swollen from the blow.*)

RAFAL: Is he asleep?

DOLFIN: Who?

RAFAL: The Captain.

DOLFIN: He's asleep.

MARCO: Who?

DOLFIN: The Captain.

RAFAL: I knew about this.

DOLFIN: Sorry?

RAFAL: I knew about the transport. Months ago.

DOLFIN: You're saying –

RAFAL: I wanted to be part of it despite my delicate constitution. Convinced the judges with some sleight of hand.

DOLFIN: The transport?

RAFAL: It wasn't hard.

COCCO: (*waking up more*) Wait a second, wait a second, though.

DOLFIN: Shh.

COCCO: What do you mean sleight of hand?

DOLFIN: Why?

RAFAL: I have a plan.

DOLFIN: You have a – ?

RAFAL: To steal the painting and still deliver it. (*They all stare at him. The boy smiles.*) I am a trained magician.

COCCO: What does that have to do with anything?

RAFAL: Oh, believe me.

DOLFIN: Can we see a little something?

(*Rafal steps into the fire and disappears. Dolfin and Cocco see he's missing, but Marco has dropped off to sleep.*)

COCCO: Where'd he go?

DOLFIN: He's here.

COCCO: Marco, wake up.

MARCO: Huh?

COCCO: Rafal has disappeared.

(*Marco starts.*)

DOLFIN: No, no! He means on purpose. He disappeared on purpose.

MARCO: I don't understand.

DOLFIN: He performed a trick.

(*Rafal reappears.*)

RAFAL: I'm also an expert counterfeiter.

MARCO: He's back.

COCCO: Don't scare us like that.

DOLFIN: Sorry, you're a what?

RAFAL: Counterfeiter. A forger. I have a buyer for the painting and the materials to copy it. The buyer lives in a castle three days east of here. Everything has been arranged. All we have to do is –

DOLFIN: Three days east? Isn't that getting awfully close to the Turk?

RAFAL: He is a Turk.

DOLFIN: Who?

RAFAL: My buyer.

DOLFIN: Oh no.

MARCO: No, no.

RAFAL: All right, he's not exactly a Turk. But a foreigner. Very foreign. He's very rich, aesthetic and discerning.

MARCO: No no no.

RAFAL: The emperor is a foreigner too. What, you love this foreigner more than that foreigner?

MARCO: That foreigner is a heathen.

RAFAL: The emperor is a heathen too. Rudolf? I told you. He collects conjurers who call forth devils to stand before him. He peers through telescopes at the stars, perceiving them closely in all their nakedness.

MARCO: I thought you liked the emperor.

RAFAL: Godless man, Marco. But a buyer is a buyer.

BORROMEO: He said that? A buyer is a buyer?

DOLFIN: Do you want me to finish telling it like it was, or not?

BORROMEO: I'm merely seeking to clarif–

DOLFIN: You weren't there. Look at you. Interrupting the scene as if you were there!

BORROMEO: I had forgotten you were an actor.

DOLFIN: Calcinate! Lixiviate! Get out of the scene!

BORROMEO: (*stepping aside*) My apologies.

(*But Councillor Zen has been revealed behind him.*)

DOLFIN: You too?

ZEN: I saw fit to step in.

DOLFIN: This is unacceptable.

BORROMEO: I'm sorry, Signore Dolfin.

ZEN: I assure you, I'm only here for your protection –

DOLFIN: Avaunt!

(*Zen recedes and the scene continues.*)

MARCO: You talk too fast, you talk too fast!

RAFAL: I'm excited.

MARCO: What do you want me to do?

RAFAL: Just listen. Once we've slipped our escort, then we get to the castle, and then you can all –

DOLFIN: What castle?

RAFAL: My buyer's castle! And then you all simply have to lie low while I make a copy of the painting to deliver to the emperor.

DOLFIN: Are you so talented?

RAFAL: I dare say I can improve on the original.

MARCO: But it's the Baby Jesus.

RAFAL: That's not so hard. He's all everyone wants painted these days. For hundreds of years, your artists kept all the Greek and Roman gods alive through their painting. And then that old windbag Luther comes along, and what happens? Now we paint Jesus and more Jesus and Mary and Joseph and the apostles and the Book of Revelation.

DOLFIN: So much anger for a child.

RAFAL: I am a wise child.

COCCO: He's no scrub. I was slaughtering Turks at his age. I was in the Battle of Lepan–

DOLFIN: Don't change the subject!

RAFAL: Marco. Four months I studied this painting. I would hide behind the altar until everyone went away. I made sketches, studies. In the end, we'll have become richer than Croesus –

MARCO: I need to sleep now. We should sleep.
(*Silence for a moment.*)
What do you mean richer?

RAFAL: My buyer is willing to pay three times the emperor's price.

DOLFIN: You're dreaming.

RAFAL: I have it in writing.

COCCO: Not on you, I hope.

DOLFIN: How do you plan to escape from the Captain?

RAFAL: Him? He's a pushover.

MARCO: We are talking this like real now?

DOLFIN: We've been talking it the whole time.

RAFAL: We've been implementing it the whole time.

MARCO: I –

RAFAL: Your life is precarious, Marco. You live in a floating city.

MARCO: This is worse than that.

RAFAL: Marco. When we're standing before the emperor, it will all get swept away.

MARCO: How?

RAFAL: (*acting the part*) Your Imperial Majesty, we were set upon by a band of marauding Turks! They took us; they enslaved us; they pried open our crate! But as soon as our humble Marco clapped eyes upon this vision of the Holy Virgin Mother of God, why, he summoned the strength of Roland and vanquished the foe, fourteen in a single blow and then another seven with the second, leaving only the black-bearded pasha to gape and flee into his own lands. And he had a story to tell, Emperor, of the sort of Christian man he might find within your borders. Not to mention the sort of art!

(*Marco has been laughing and making the sign of the cross all through this.*)

MARCO: You talk so fast. You think he will believe this?

CAPTAIN: (*starting*) Shut up!

(*The Captain goes back to sleep.*)

RAFAL: My friend, we are Venetians. Are we not the greatest lying, thieving rascals on the whole of the earth?

DOLFIN: (*to Borromeo*) Now and that's the point, isn't it? We are. The greatest lying, thieving rascals on the whole of the earth, from the Indies to the – oh, wait. I've just confessed to the plotting of a crime, haven't I.

BORROMEO: You have.

DOLFIN: Your Eminence, it was all just – talk.

BORROMEO: Indeed.

DOLFIN: We never would have carried it out.

BORROMEO: Tell me, how was the boy planning to give the Captain the slip?

DOLFIN: But have you not guessed?

BORROMEO: Sorry?

DOLFIN: Magic, Your Eminence. Tricks! Misdirection! With a little help from (*gesturing up*) 'the gods.'

BORROMEO: The gods?

DOLFIN: That's what my master used to call them. My master had a few powders, very mild, to make the audience a little more persuadable, malleable; he gave me a little mortar and pestle, palm-sized. All I'd have to do? *Achoo!* The only problem was they'd hit me hardest and I'd end up falling off the upturned cart while trying to peel off my pantaloons. Why I wanted to peel off my pantaloons I could never quite –

BORROMEO: Signore –

DOLFIN: Eminence, I'm convinced that boy had an apothecary up his sleeve. Far better than mine. Believe me. You paint a picture in the air in front of you and I could swear I see it. I could *swear*.

BORROMEO: But his hands were bound. How could he sneeze into – ?

DOLFIN: Into his collar then. I'm telling you, Eminence. I know the type. I am the type. He's better than me though, that's for sure. And when he got into a bind, he pulled from his bag of – (*the floor*) There's blood here. On the floor.

BORROMEO: That's not my fault.

DOLFIN: I didn't say it was your fault, I just said it was here.

BORROMEO: Don't look at it.

DOLFIN: It's right at my feet!

BORROMEO: He pulled from his bag of tricks, you say.

DOLFIN: (*starting to panic*) I thought you were I thought you were – I always think the best of people. But you've got killers in your employ. Cocco, for example. He's a professional soldier, willing to lay aside any scruples for a ducat or two, I know my life can't be worth much more than –

BORROMEO: Signore Dolfin!
        You've been very helpful. Thank you for your deposition.

DOLFIN: I –

BORROMEO: There's the door.

DOLFIN: But –

BORROMEO: The door.

DOLFIN: You're not going to kill me?

BORROMEO: No.

DOLFIN: And Signore Cocco is not going to kill me?

BORROMEO: Certainly not.

DOLFIN: Anyone else?

BORROMEO: No!

DOLFIN: Councillor Zen?

BORROMEO: The door.

DOLFIN: (*approaches the door*) Well ... Forgive me, but ... I must say ... if I may ... I'm not finished.

BORROMEO: I beg your pardon?

DOLFIN: I've got lots of other things you might want to hear.

BORROMEO: You do?

DOLFIN: But if you want me to go. If you need a chance to catch your breath or bring in a housekeeper or, or a mason –

BORROMEO: No no.

DOLFIN: You're sure.

BORROMEO: Please stay.

DOLFIN: Very well.

BORROMEO: You look so pleased.

DOLFIN: Well, I left out the best part. The juicy part. A man likes to be discreet about certain things, you know? I'm not sure what's right.

BORROMEO: Signore.

DOLFIN: You see, Eminence, the thing is: I believe our boy had fallen in love.

BORROMEO: Love?

DOLFIN: Are you not familiar with 'love,' Your Emin– ?

BORROMEO: Try to refrain from patronizing me, Signore. I may not be violent, and I may be a cleric, but I do have feelings.

DOLFIN: I'm – so sorry. Don't kill me?

BORROMEO: How love? When?

DOLFIN: Same night. Just earlier. Before he told us his plan.

> (*The scene. Night. Camp. The Captain is asleep by his own fire a small distance away. Rafal is talking to Dolfin and Marco about Rudolf and the stars.*)

RAFAL: The emperor peers through telescopes at the stars. Though they'd rather be left alone.

COCCO: The stars are on to something. Some of us are trying to SLEEP.

DOLFIN: Cocco. We know your bark is worse than your bite.

COCCO: You have no idea about my bite. Hold up now, let me look at that eye. Captain hit you pretty hard.

DOLFIN: You can't lip a man like that.

RAFAL: He tried to steal the painting.

COCCO: Let me see.

RAFAL: It's nothing.

COCCO: It's swollen shut. Here. (*He pulls a small dagger from his shoe.*)

RAFAL: Cocco conceals a weapon.

COCCO: Cocco is no fool.

DOLFIN: Cocco's an assassin.

RAFAL: Are you going to kill me?

COCCO: I'm going to have to cut right here. (*just above the eye*)

RAFAL: Why?

COCCO: There's blood pumping in there that's got no place to go. Your eye is going to pop out if we don't do something.

RAFAL: But if you cut it, won't the blood come out?

COCCO: Better out than in.

RAFAL: If it falls out, I'll never get it back!

COCCO: The eye?

RAFAL: The blood!

COCCO: No. Your body will make more.

RAFAL: You know that do you?

COCCO: (*lifting his shirt*) You see this scar? I know.

RAFAL: Oh ... very well. But careful.

COCCO: Don't worry.

RAFAL: I mean my blood could harm you, it's like poison.

COCCO: What a kid you are.

RAFAL: I'm serious.

COCCO: I'm sure you are.

RAFAL: I'll refuse.

COCCO: All right! Look that way. (*He turns his head with his hand.*) Better?

RAFAL: Just be careful.

COCCO: Hold still.

(*There is a spurt of blood.*)

RAFAL: Oh! Disgusting! Careful, Cocco!

COCCO: Didn't touch me.

RAFAL: Everybody stay away!

COCCO: You can see better now, no?

DOLFIN: Cocco is a doctor.

COCCO: Just a veteran.

RAFAL: Oh look at the stars. I suppose they approve I have both eyes back.
(*as if addressing the stars*) It's good that Cocco is clever.

DOLFIN: Cocco was clever.

BORROMEO: You believe that the boy loved Cocco?

DOLFIN: I believe it was mutual.

BORROMEO: How could you tell?

DOLFIN: May I present the first lovers' spat.

(*The scene. Dolfin is trying to defend the painting from the point of view of the artist.*)

COCCO: Now, who will stand in for the artist?

DOLFIN: What? No!

BORROMEO: I know this story.

DOLFIN: Yes. The night they all decided to humiliate me.

BORROMEO: Humiliate you?

DOLFIN: People love to humiliate me. I'm an actor. Sometimes I like to make people laugh. So people think that means they can laugh at me whenever they choose.

BORROMEO: I still don't –

DOLFIN: They made me play the painter!
(*He transitions back to the scene, playing the artist.*)
My name is Albrecht Dürer. I'm an artist. This is my canvas.

MARCO: It's not a canvas, it's poplar wood.

DOLFIN: You see that?

BORROMEO: Signore –

COCCO: Doesn't matter if it's canvas or poplar wood. To the iconoclast, both will burn just as bright.

CAPTAIN: How do you know so much, soldier?

COCCO: I spent many months destroying art.

RAFAL: *You* did that?

COCCO: The money was very good.

CAPTAIN: Cover that up.

(*Cocco covers the painting with help from Dolfin and Marco.*)

DOLFIN: The soldier knows about art.

RAFAL: The soldier is a doctor who knows about art. He has spent some time devoted to its destruction.

COCCO: You learn a lot about a thing by taking it apart. Whether that thing be the human anatomy or the depth of a brush-stroke by Leonardo.

RAFAL: You've destroyed Leonardo?

COCCO: It was a figure of speech.

RAFAL: No it wasn't.

COCCO: It was a long time ago.

RAFAL: You destroyed work by Leonardo da Vinci!

CAPTAIN: The most beloved painter of all time.

COCCO: Truthfully, I don't know for sure.

RAFAL: Yes you do. What was it?

COCCO: What was what?

RAFAL: The da Vinci you destroyed?

COCCO: Oh ... if it really was –

RAFAL: It was.

COCCO: It was a depiction of the young – er –

RAFAL: John the Baptist?

COCCO: How would you know that?

RAFAL: Leonardo only called it John the Baptist, it was really Dionysos!

COCCO: I wouldn't know anything about that.

CAPTAIN: Because you're just a soldier.

RAFAL: I thought you were a bright light. A star in my earth-bound firmament. But you're just another ignorant soldier –

COCCO: No!

RAFAL: – setting fire to towns and raping women and boys!

(*The Captain has withdrawn.*)

COCCO: I'm nothing of the sort!

RAFAL: I thought I could trust the three of you at least.

MARCO: You can trust me.

DOLFIN: And me.

COCCO: Oh thank you, my friends, all my good friends, thank you so much.

DOLFIN: Two out of three. Not that bad.

COCCO: I fixed your eye. Give a kid back his sight and what does he do?

RAFAL: He sees.

COCCO: Oh good.

DOLFIN: Kid, you really can trust me. I'm with you all the way.

COCCO: You think the boy is going to save you somehow? Because last I checked he wasn't the second coming of the Messiah.

DOLFIN: He has a concrete plan.

COCCO: He said he was a magician.

DOLFIN: Yes, and –

RAFAL: (*pointing to Cocco*) *He* said he was an iconoclast.

COCCO: Former –

RAFAL: – of the first order.

COCCO: – and for pay.

RAFAL: Even worse.

DOLFIN: I just want you to go through with your plan. It's a good plan, I can help you, let me be your apprentice, I'm a quick study, I've got talented fingers, I can learn –

RAFAL: I'm going to sleep.

(*He settles in. Dolfin glares at Cocco*)

COCCO: I can't help what the kid thinks.

DOLFIN: You could have kept your mouth shut!

COCCO: He's not going to help you!

DOLFIN: He has a buyer!

COCCO: He has a buyer and you can't see what's happening right in front of your big nose!

BORROMEO: What did he mean by that?

DOLFIN: I felt he was insulting my nose.

COCCO: And I certainly don't conceal my past because it's inconvenient for people to hear about it.

DOLFIN: But he adores you. You might have known he would have been offended by your –

COCCO: What am I supposed to do? Tell me, Dolfin, what am I supposed to do to make it up to him? I'm all ears.

DOLFIN: ...
(*to Borromeo*) When a man like that turns to me for ideas, I know we're in trouble.

They didn't speak to one another for three days. People are simple, Your Eminence. We always think it's popes and kings and courts and priests who make the world go round. But it's not. It's love and hate and desire and pride.

And tricks. At least when we finally came to the Village of –

COCCO: (*in the church*) I was in the Battle of Lepanto.

BORROMEO: – Pusterwald –

DOLFIN: – where they were going to burn us for our beliefs –

COCCO: I was there.

DOLFIN: – but then our brilliant boy got smitten all over again –

COCCO: Give me some credit.

DOLFIN: – when Cocco spoke.

BORROMEO: Smitten? I thought –

COCCO: The Great Holy League coming together to defeat the Turk.

BORROMEO: I thought the boy made fun of Cocco when he spoke.

COCCO: The Battle of Lepanto. You all know what we did. I fought hand to hand on their ships, none of your faraway cannons that you have today. Hand to hand. Eye to eye. I was seventeen years old. I didn't know anything. We rammed those ships together, pulled out our swords and leapt into a slick, creaky, sinking battlefield.

My friend here, Marco, he's an oarmaker. Our sails weren't as good as they are today, so without his oars, the Turk would be standing here in our places.

MARCO: What?

DOLFIN: Shh.

MARCO: But he's saying I was –

DOLFIN: Shh!

COCCO: I came upon a sick man there, on that Musselman deck. His eyes had a hollow look, his mouth twisted in pain. I thought he was possessed – a man with a bloated belly, wasting away. 'Why, it must be the devil sitting in there!' Like you all with this crate: there's a devil in there!

I faced that man and I sliced him open. And it wasn't the devil that came out. The thing in him did not come from his sins or the fact that he was a Turk. It was an ague of the liver I think. It pisses fluid into his belly and swells it up. That's real. These devils aren't real. That's real. And that man did not deserve to be killed by me. He didn't even have the strength to lift his sword. He deserved to be nestled in the comfort of his family. Not to be butchered surrounded

81

on both sides by people who understood nothing about him. I say this even though I am a Christian and he a Musselman. Look me in the eye if you've seen your own mother die from such a disease and tell me you would wish that on anyone. These fateful things are governed by chance. Yet we waste so much time on gods.

RAFAL: Should they have helped their people more?

COCCO: There were other things I saw in those wars that wiser men will prove one day. Then we'll all know. Like, I believe the blood flows through the body. Not by the grace of God but rather a constant clenching of the heart, like *this* and like *this* and like *this*. It flows away and back again. I've seen it. Use your hearts now. Not your minds. All we are is men. Labourers. Let us go. It brings no good to anyone for men to destroy the works of other men.

RAFAL: You don't know how to talk to these people, Cocco. Trying to show them a heart and making it slow down. Trying to make them change the way they feel! The devil loves that kind of talk.

DOLFIN: The boy was in love again. And so: POOF! He riled up that crowd and gave them a trick, to save us all, when he could have slipped through the *peroledi* and saved himself.

BORROMEO: What on earth is the *peroledi*?

DOLFIN: Oh. Sorry. The layers of the air.

BORROMEO: I see. Alchemy. One trick instead of another.

DOLFIN: Poof.

After that, the people of Pusterwald loved us too – loved us so much they wanted to keep us, so they put us in the church for the night. Locked the door. We were still prisoners!

BORROMEO: Until the Venetian army came.

DOLFIN: (*with a flourish*) Yes, until the army came and set us free.

BORROMEO: So you're finished.

DOLFIN: No. Oh no. I have more. A little more. I can tell you more. There was one more trick he did. It was a little trick but it was a good trick. While we were locked in that church. I'm not sure the others even saw it. But I couldn't figure it out though. Those little ones, they're always the hardest.

> (*The scene in the church. After the miracle. Night. They are no longer bound. The Captain is not there. Rafal is pounding on the door, he sports a garland, carries a wineskin and behaves as if he is drunk.*)

RAFAL: Let us out of here! Let us out!

DOLFIN: Is that wine you've got?

RAFAL: Don't you have some?

DOLFIN: No.

RAFAL: Liar.

DOLFIN: I don't have wine!

RAFAL: What's in your flask?

DOLFIN: Water!

RAFAL: Let me see. (*Tastes it.*) Water. Dolfin drank all the wine.

DOLFIN: I did not drink all the wine! I didn't drink any wine.

RAFAL: I didn't drink any wine.

DOLFIN: Look at you. You're still drinking it.

RAFAL: Oh, we're really stuck here.

DOLFIN: Was there wine and I missed it?

RAFAL: If they respected our relic, you'd think they'd respect its destiny. To find its way to Prague. Not linger in some piss-poor town like this. (*He thumps on door, gets tired quickly.*)

Oh, my friends. Let's not be sad. You're all so much better than I thought men could ever be. Allow me to present you to the stars as three good men. Stars, look upon them: here is Marco, who will stand up to the strong on behalf of the weak. Show him respect.

And Cocco. I forget what's so great about Cocco. I forget. It cannot have been very important.

But Dolfin. Like our own little Rudolf, right here in this little world. He doesn't know what to believe, so he believes everything.

DOLFIN: I do?

RAFAL: I invoke the stars to honour him.

DOLFIN: We can't see the stars in here.

RAFAL: I can always see the stars.

And then Cocco. I didn't really forget. With his medicine like a miracle. The movement of the blood, the disease of the liver. The healing of my eye. The future. In the old days, gods walked the earth and flew above it, turning women into bears and trees and men into stags and flowers and madmen who could get torn apart by their own mad mothers. A lot of human blood was shed. I think Cocco could have staunched some of it.

Perhaps the gods were too cruel to the people. They had no idea how frail they were. The gods were frail! How they required your attention! Your love. Some would destroy the gods, like the Captain. But Cocco somehow saves them, with his all-too-human art. Here is Cocco. He is clever. Show him honour.

MARCO: Clever.

COCCO: I'm not clever, kid. I just noticed a thing or two by chance.

RAFAL: If you say so.

DOLFIN: I notice things too. I noticed: the kid didn't give me any wine.

RAFAL: Oh here, Dolfin, give it to me.

DOLFIN: What?

RAFAL: Give me your flask. If I can't do this, I might as well lie down and die. (*He tastes it, spits in it, gives it back to Dolfin.*) There. Try it now.

DOLFIN: You just spit in it!

RAFAL: Taste!

DOLFIN: You spat in it.

RAFAL: (*calmly*) Taste.

(*Dolfin tastes. Zen enters.*)

RAFAL: (*He retrieves the flask, drinking from it as he withdraws.*) A fine Pusterwaldian vintage.

ZEN: I've never been partial to the grape.

BORROMEO: Councillor –

(*Dolfin is alone again, with Borromeo and Zen.*)

ZEN: Archbishop. I simply wanted to ensure that Signore Dolfin made it safely to the end of his interview. I'm fond of him. I was fond of the Captain, too. Zealous man. Tell me again what he said about doing falsehood?

BORROMEO: The Captain said all who do falsehood should have their throats slit.

ZEN: And then he slit his own throat. What miracles a miracle brings. Where will it stop? Rumours of further miracles, perhaps? The healing of the sick? The raising of the dead? Water into wine? Venetians embracing the pope, embarking on pilgrimages, ceasing all work? Destroying the unique secular nature of our state?

DOLFIN: I didn't think it was a miracle. I told him –

ZEN: Hush now.

BORROMEO: Well, Councillor, as you can see, Signore Dolfin is all right.

ZEN: I'm glad. I did have one question for him: How he feels about the painting.

DOLFIN: Me? I don't know what you mean.

ZEN: The painting, Signore. How do you feel about it? Do you like it?

DOLFIN: Do I like it? It's … well, it's a very – colourful –

ZEN: You see these two men, Signore? (*the pope and the emperor*) They formed an alliance of church and state against Venice.

DOLFIN: I always thought it was an ugly painting.

ZEN: Honestly?

DOLFIN: These Germans: they slap colours on a canvas but they don't know how to paint like a Venetian can paint. I don't know how he ever got away with painting it here in the first place.

ZEN: Thank you, Signore. The Council can use the talents of a man like you.

BORROMEO: What does this prove, Councillor?

ZEN: Nothing at all, Archbishop. I'm simply asking questions and receiving answers.

BORROMEO: Indeed.

ZEN: And displaying for your benefit what an exemplary Venetian our Signore Dolfin is. Shall we make our way, Signore? We wouldn't want the cardinal archbishop to feel he's wasting his time with this inquiry.

ACT TWO, SCENE TWO

(*Borromeo and Cocco. Perhaps Borromeo has set up two ornate prayer benches facing each other, each with its own matching pointer.*)

BORROMEO: You have a stutter.

COCCO: ...

BORROMEO: Your compatriots have told me it is non-existent in their company.

COCCO: ...

BORROMEO: Yes. I wonder if we might conduct a little experiment to mitigate my authority.

COCCO: You want me to f-forget that I'm d-d-d-d–? (*gesturing slitting his throat*)

BORROMEO: I don't know what you've heard, Signore, but I will guarantee your safety. Now, do you know what this painting is meant to convey? The Brotherhood of the Rosary, founded in 1475: as reputable as the Venetian Council of Ten, only anyone can join, as an equal. There may be rank before the father or the son but never before the mother. All these men and women – old, young, rich, poor, a pope, an emperor, a cardinal, a soldier – are equal.

Look at the painting, Signore. You and I are going to have a conversation. I propose we imagine, not that I am this cardinal (*points*) and you are this soldier (*points*), but rather that I am this pope (*points*) and you are this emperor. That way, at least there won't be all these people in the way.

COCCO: ...

BORROMEO: Within the painting, we are equals.

COCCO: I'm not a child. I have k-illed.

BORROMEO: I know it. Try it?

COCCO: This is s-s-s-t–

BORROMEO: Now, do you have anything to say about the placement of the boy among your ranks in the strongman competition?

COCCO: That's a very nice robe you've got. So much nicer than mine. Where did you get it?

BORROMEO: I don't know.

COCCO: It looks Venetian.

BORROMEO: Perhaps you could answer the question?

COCCO: Too busy.

BORROMEO: Busy with what?

COCCO: Praying.

BORROMEO: Not too busy to comment on the colours in my robe. Without a stutter.

COCCO: Does it not b-bore you to hear the same story over and over again from different people?

BORROMEO: I am accustomed to the form.

COCCO: What form.

BORROMEO: It is the structure of the gospels.

COCCO: I don't know how the kid did it. I did not see. But, as I myself can p-prove, p-people are vulnerable in unex-pected ways. So why can they not be strong in unexpected ways?

BORROMEO: So he lifted the cart full of cabbages?

COCCO: I did not see it.

BORROMEO: Tell me about him.

COCCO: What's there to tell? He's just a kid. He has delusions, he's just a kid.

BORROMEO: What do you mean he has delusions?

COCCO: Your Emin– Your Holiness, I mean childish delusions. Remember when you were a child, insert the things you might have imagined about yourself then, and let that be my answer.

BORROMEO: When I was a child, I imagined being a bishop and an art collector. I imagined feeding the poor and defending the sick against death. I imagined forgiving former witches without recourse to the flame and bringing them back to the fold, going so far as to house and clothe them. I imagined building a gallery. I imagined writing books.

COCCO: Have you done all that?

BORROMEO: By the grace of God.

COCCO: Even the bit with the witches?

BORROMEO: Still working on the housing. Difficult to convince my superiors of its merit.

COCCO: How did you come to see its merit?

BORROMEO: Personal reasons.

COCCO: Is that all I'm going to get?

BORROMEO: Yes.

COCCO: So you were a clear-thinking child.

BORROMEO: Signore Dolfin says the boy was in love with you.

COCCO: Signore Dolfin comes from the stage.

BORROMEO: The boy was not in love with you?

COCCO: The boy, as you call him –

BORROMEO: Did you not just call him a boy?

COCCO: I called him a kid.

BORROMEO: What's the difference?

COCCO: Sometimes I thought he was as old as the wind. But it was foolish for the Venetian Council of Ten, d-despite their most serene wisdom, to allow him on our expedition.

He's handsome, intelligent and frail. F-full of curiosity and de-fiance and lack of f-fear for his betters. Not his betters but those who are merely stronger than him. In such crude company as ours, the man with all the power was bound to grease him up and abuse him.

BORROMEO: (*sign of the cross*) Horrible.

COCCO: Oh, leave it behind, Father. You're a priest. Surely you've heard of pederasty.

BORROMEO: I'll thank you to address me as 'Your Eminence.'

COCCO: (*trying to remain defiant*) But you said th-th-th-th-th-that we w-w-w-w-w–

BORROMEO: You think members of the clergy engage in abusing innocent children? I think you could have more respect for my station. I think that would be wise.

COCCO: P-p-p-p-p-p–

BORROMEO: Oh stop it.

COCCO: N-n-n-n-n-n–

BORROMEO: The painting, Cocco. You have nothing to fear from me.

COCCO: I c-c-c–

BORROMEO: I'm sorry. The painting.

COCCO: W-w–

BORROMEO: I suppose I should be addressing you as your most Imperial and Royal Majesty, King of Bohemia, Margrave of Moravia, Prince of Piombino, King of Hungary, Croatia, and Slavonia, Archduke of Austria, King of the Romans. Is that better?

COCCO: Surprisingly effective.

BORROMEO: So, the man with the power – you mean the Captain – was violent with the boy and also, you say, he s-sodomized the boy.

COCCO: I am too coarse.

BORROMEO: But this is completely new information. Not a hint of it so far.

COCCO: I'm a soldier. I've seen plenty of things that people do not speak of.

BORROMEO: I really don't know how to proceed. It would be my preference to call the Captain back for questioning.

COCCO: Why don't you?

BORROMEO: It can't be done.

COCCO: Venetians, yeah? Sticklers for form.

BORROMEO: Signore Dolfin believed the boy was trying to get away from the Captain because he had a Turkish buyer for the painting.

COCCO: Did he now. (*laughs*) A Turkish buyer. Oh, Signore Dolfin.

BORROMEO: The boy did not speak of a buyer?

COCCO: Signore Dolfin cannot tell the difference between the truth and a lie.

As I've said, the kid wanted to get away from a man who was abusing him.

BORROMEO: A Landsknecht Captain.

COCCO: And he didn't trust the rest of us with something as simple as the truth. So he came up with the lie that would seem to bring us gain. A Turkish buyer. A brilliant forgery that he would paint with his skill. If we had gone with him to find that Turkish buyer, he would have come up with a story about how that Turkish buyer had died or disappeared or was going to betray us to the sultan so we better get away, we better get back on the road to Prague. There was no Turkish buyer, Eminence. All that kid wanted was to give a cruel man the slip and make it alive with this precious cargo to his beloved city of Prague. I wish I could have helped him. I wish I'd let the Captain take the painting when he wanted to.

BORROMEO: You don't think the Captain would have destroyed the painting?

COCCO: I know they say he set up the trap in Pusterwald. But the kid never would've parted with it anyway, even for a few days; he was like a dog with a bone with the painting. He would've carried it all the way to Prague by himself if he had to. He had a plan for it, like, a different plan: I don't know what it was but I'm sure it was something. He really thought he was something, something s-special; s-something like –

BORROMEO: Yes?

COCCO: I told you: he had childish delusions.

BORROMEO: Yes but what delusions?

COCCO: Why did you seek to protect the witches?

BORROMEO: I'm not going to tell you.

COCCO: Your Holiness, you must promise to protect the kid: you must promise to let him get to Prague and you must promise me Rafal will not end up standing before –

BORROMEO: Who?

COCCO: (*St. Dominic*) Men like that. With their fetters.

BORROMEO: Signore, this is not Spain.

COCCO: I'll thank you to address me as your most imperial and royal majesty.

BORROMEO: I'm sorry.

COCCO: Your own Roman Inquisition burned a man five years ago.

BORROMEO: It was six years ago, not five.

COCCO: I see. What was his name?

BORROMEO: It doesn't matter.

COCCO: Bruno, or – someth–

BORROMEO: That was a dangerous heretic.

COCCO: (*referring to the painting*) So I guess he's not in here then. The brotherhood of equals.

BORROMEO: Anyway, this is Venice –

COCCO: Swear to me, before God, the Blessed Virgin and child and our Brotherhood of the Rosary; Rafal will not end up standing before Inquisitors.

BORROMEO: Can we not just – ?

COCCO: Or I will remain as close-mouthed as all assembled here.

BORROMEO: Very well. I swear to protect the boy to the best of my ability.

COCCO: Beyond your best ability. It means striking some of what I say from your report.

BORROMEO: What if I am bound to make a complete report?

COCCO: Then you are in a double bind. Your report is incomplete either way, but in one case you'll hear the whole truth.

BORROMEO: One moment.
   (*He goes to check the door, perhaps even going right out. No one is there.*)
   All right, I swear. He's just a boy.

COCCO: Who believes he is the Greek g-god, Dio-Dionysos.

BORROMEO: Dionysos?

COCCO: Yes, Your Holiness.

BORROMEO: But that doesn't make any sense.

COCCO: Why not?

BORROMEO: Dionysos. He told you that.

COCCO: No, but he hinted at it all the time. He thought his blood was poison to men. It's what the ancients believed. He addressed the stars as if they were his family. He had strong feelings for certain paintings.

BORROMEO: What paintings?

COCCO: (*shrugs*) Classical themes.

BORROMEO: But what about this painting?

COCCO: I don't know.

BORROMEO: But this is the painting in question, is it not?

COCCO: I –

BORROMEO: After all, he was said to have brought the Virgin Mary out of this painting.

COCCO: Yes.

BORROMEO: Mother of Jesus, no association with Dionysos. An utterly Christian painting.

COCCO: Your Holiness, I see your point, but –

BORROMEO: Your charge is heresy.

COCCO: Well, you can burn me if you like, but for him you swore an oath. Anyway, it's not heresy. He's a frail kid, he just wants to feel strong: 'I *think* I am a *god*, therefore *I am strong.*'

BORROMEO: But why *that* god? Why Dionysos?

COCCO: You're asking me?

BORROMEO: It's your theory.

COCCO: You're asking me where he got the idea? I don't know; I don't keep track of these things. The way the young people – think these days. Well, except ...

BORROMEO: Yes?

COCCO: I could speculate. You won't like it.
       That man you burnt –

BORROMEO: This again.

COCCO: Did he not have similar delusions? About the gods and the stars?

BORROMEO: His ideas were not as influential as all that.

COCCO: Why'd you burn him then?

BORROMEO: I –

COCCO: When something as powerful as the Roman church burns a man at the stake, aren't you saying his ideas are powerful? Aren't you saying they're interesting? That's what I would think, if I was young.

BORROMEO: That thinking would bring you nothing but trouble.

COCCO: Trouble. How alluring.

BORROMEO: All right. All right. But what of the miracle?

COCCO: What of it?

BORROMEO: Tell me about it.

COCCO: Oh come on, Your Holiness. I'm really not interested.

BORROMEO: This is the sole purpose of this inquiry. What did you see?

COCCO: What do you think I saw?

BORROMEO: The Virgin came out of the painting, yes?

COCCO: Astounding. You could have been there yourself.

BORROMEO: Oh shut up. And did he sneeze?

COCCO: Who?

BORROMEO: The boy?

COCCO: Sneeze! How should I know?

BORROMEO: You're not the least bit interested in how the Virgin was made to move.

COCCO: What makes you think it really happened?

BORROMEO: Fifty-six people saw it. Didn't you?

COCCO: What did the others see?

BORROMEO: They all saw the same thing. What did you see?

COCCO: Likely what they saw.

BORROMEO: Really.

COCCO: I can't explain it, Your Holiness. Somebody will, someday. Wiser –

BORROMEO: *Try.*

COCCO: ... We're standing there, Eminence. A crowd of people thinks the devil is in a box, massive, evil. The crowd, too: evil. We're in some kind of trouble. I raise up my beating heart and throw it down. But it's no good. The stupid kid is whipping them up. They're going to tear us apart. Then the box opens. There she is. (*points at the painting*) Look at her. Fifty-six breaths catch in fifty-six throats. Us too. When you expect the devil and you see that ... well ... But then it goes *further*, because even *that* is wrong. That. Wrong. That. Another kind of delusion. So now: look at *that* and try to think: death; destruction; mayhem; horror. Can you? Pusterwaldian? You must.

And then the boy catches our attention. We look away, to him, and back again. And then ...

BORROMEO: And then?

COCCO: Hope. Tears. Joy. Beauty. Delusion.

BORROMEO: Veneration of the Virgin is delusion?

COCCO: When she comes to life, that's delusion. I'd venture to say: Dionysian.

BORROMEO: Have I another heretic here?

COCCO: (*shrugs*) Art has power, Your Holiness. You must know that. You proved it yourself, right here with me.

BORROMEO: How?

COCCO: A pope and an emperor, Eminence. A pope and an emperor.

BORROMEO: Oh that, but that was simply –

COCCO: Simply what?

BORROMEO: Just ... simply ...

COCCO: What? I'm curious how you plan to diminish your swift remedy for my lifelong affliction, miraculously employing art.

BORROMEO: It's not the same!

COCCO: It is the same. It's a miracle. Art makes miracles.

BORROMEO: Signore, you have been mocked here today for your impediment.

COCCO: Councilor Zen was not wrong to mock me, Eminence. I am a mockable man.

BORROMEO: I find you rather eloquent.

COCCO: I'm eloquent before grunts, murderers, iconoclasts, charlatans and these painted people, which is the same as not being eloquent at all.

BORROMEO: Well, I intend to raise you up.

COCCO: I'm sorry?

BORROMEO: This city: I've noticed she is ever vigilant in matters of public health, undertaking massive projects in its name.

COCCO: It's true.

BORROMEO: Well, Signore, I will recommend that you be posted to the commission that oversees such matters. To see what you can learn there. What you can *do* there.

COCCO: Your Eminence. I am not a young man.

BORROMEO: But you are a capable one. Clearly. The world is often blind to a man's virtues. In this instance, I refuse to let that blindness stand.

COCCO: I –

BORROMEO: Do you have any objections?

COCCO: No, Your Eminence.

BORROMEO: Good. And I can only hope, Signore, that it's merely a matter of time before you will see yourself as the equal of any you address.

COCCO: (*bows*) I t-trust you'll stick to your v-vow.

ACT TWO, SCENE THREE

(*The strong men are carrying their burden in the mountains – the usual set-up with the Captain marching beside. Rafal is looking off into space, dreamily, though it is a struggle for him. When Cocco speaks, he's brought back to the present.*)

COCCO: Heavy!

RAFAL: Oh ...

COCCO: Urgh!

RAFAL: Can you see how tired I am, Eminence? How weak?

BORROMEO: Yes, I can.

COCCO: Who will lighten my mood!

RAFAL: It's been a long road, Eminence.

BORROMEO: Would you like me to lend you a shoulder?

RAFAL: Ha! No. Thank you, but I would not miss this time in the mountains for whole of the world below or the stars above.

(*Marco leads a song as they march: 'The Reaping Song' from* Lyrichord's Work Songs, Volume 1, Folk Music and Songs of Sicily. [Sheet music appears on p. 117] *As they finish, Rafal falls again and Marco comes to help him. The others have to carry him to the camp.*)

RAFAL: These men are all so good to me. Will you be good to me, Eminence?

BORROMEO: How should I be good to you?

RAFAL: Believe me when I tell you ...

BORROMEO: When you tell me what?

RAFAL: I made a miracle.

BORROMEO: I did not have the advantage, like these others, of seeing with my own eyes.

RAFAL: These others? Did they believe what they saw? Tell me. Oh, did they? I know Marco did. Then the Captain, who, I would imagine, came to understand, upon review, that he believed too. But then Dolfin, when I told him I was a magician –

DOLFIN: Can we see a little something?

RAFAL: (*getting up, stepping into the fire*) – he believed the only explanation he was (*trying not to sneeze*) ... ever ...

COCCO: Where'd he go?

RAFAL: (*sneezes*)

DOLFIN: He's here.

RAFAL: – given. Pardon me, I – What?

BORROMEO: (*who has been fanning himself*) Nothing.

RAFAL: (*suspicious smile*) What?

BORROMEO: Nothing.

RAFAL: And finally Cocco. I imagine whatever Cocco told you, you currently believe to be the truth.

BORROMEO: What I currently believe is that an event in Pusterwald brought fifty-six people back to the bosom of the church. I'm trying to determine whether it was a true Christian miracle.

RAFAL: Why a Christian miracle?

BORROMEO: Wh–? Christian converts. Christian painting.

RAFAL: This painting? Of a virgin mother carrying a son who is a god in her arms? A man lives a quiet life until he is thirty years old, then has three spectacular years: medicine shows and magic tricks. After his death, his devotees need to fill in the story. They look no further than an old Greek cult. The virgin mother; father a god; not magic but miracles; the descent to Hades; the resurrection.

BORROMEO: All from a Greek cult.

RAFAL: Dionysos.

BORROMEO: You are a devotee.

RAFAL: How could I be? There are no devotees left, not since the days when that sweet infant took over.

BORROMEO: So, you mean you say you … are …

RAFAL: (*nods*)

BORROMEO: How can I possibly believe you.

RAFAL: It's true, my evidence is scant. I can't even call upon the alchemist who first conjured me, in Prague, since he took me for the devil, and I tried my best to play the part.

BORROMEO: Conjured in Prague?

RAFAL: Some years ago: more than three less than ten. Maybe twenty. I landed right where I was supposed to be, an emissary from the stars to the emperor. So why did I not present myself, then, in all my glory? Because I am not a vector! I am not a hypotenuse! I have *magnitude* if not direction. I am Dionysos! And I'd just fallen from the stars – was Bacchanalia not my birthright?

BORROMEO: More than three years less than twenty.

RAFAL: The time just slipped by.

BORROMEO: Whatever did you get up to?

RAFAL: I think I must refrain from answering that, out of respect for your station.

BORROMEO: Oh.

RAFAL: Yes.

BORROMEO: I see.

RAFAL: Suffice to say, I let run the immortal sap through a disbelieving world. Stil, it was fun. How far I travelled before I finally heard the name that made me come back to my senses.

BORROMEO: What name?

RAFAL: Why, Rudolf. The Second. None of us would be here now if not for what I wanted from him. I wanted … to beg him to purchase a number of other paintings: *The Judgement of Paris* by Cranach the Elder, the Hestia tapestry from Egypt, Botticelli's *Birth of Venus*, Titian's *Bacchus and Ariadne*, the Farnese *Hercules* –

BORROMEO: That's a statue.

RAFAL: Indeed, as is Belvedere's *Apollo* and the *Narcissus* of—

BORROMEO: Leoni.

RAFAL: One thousand, five hundred and thirty-three.

BORROMEO: And how did you intend to convince him to buy these paintings?

RAFAL: I heard of a painting he wanted. A Christian painting. It had been purchased here in Venice and would make its way into his presence. Why, if I could make a virgin step out of this quaint Christian painting, for the ermperor, what wonders might I provide with an image of Minerva, or Hercules? A god to conjure other gods. What collector of curiosities would not want gods in his collection?

BORROMEO: Indeed.

RAFAL: But (*approaching the Captain*) the sad fact is, I am far too susceptible to the passions of nature to be entrusted with anything so serious as a *plan*, even if I came up with it myself.

BORROMEO: Nature?

RAFAL: Sorry? (*looking back to see that the others are asleep*)

BORROMEO: You said nature. I assume you meant your nature.

RAFAL: (*as he rouses and embraces the Captain*) All nature is my nature, Eminence. The storm that decimates the hospice is my nature. The jealous maid who plucks out the eyes of the man she loves is my nature; the Colosseums that killed the Christians and your Inquisitors who watch the heathens whipped in time to a pulse within their robes. My nature. Desire. Desire. Revenge.

(*Scene. The Captain and Rafal before sunrise, post-coital.*)

CAPTAIN: You'd best get back to the others.

RAFAL: Do we have anything to fear from you, Captain? I really don't want to have anything to fear from you on this thrilling journey to a castle in Prague.

CAPTAIN: My task: (*one finger*) to ensure this painting arrives safely. (*two fingers*) To ensure the safety of you four who carry it.

RAFAL: But what would you do if that were not your task and you had the chance?

CAPTAIN: What chance?

RAFAL: A chance to go at the painting.

CAPTAIN: This painting? Why would I hate this painting? Have you seen it?

RAFAL: Yes.

CAPTAIN: I would never say this to those men. If you repeat what I say –

RAFAL: I swear, by all the gods –

CAPTAIN: 'By all the gods.'

RAFAL: – I won't repeat it.

CAPTAIN: He made noble depictions of men in my profession. Etchings. They are, I think, beautiful. And this one too. Beautiful.

RAFAL: But it's got a pope –

CAPTAIN: This painting does no harm to anybody.

RAFAL: You love a painting.

CAPTAIN: I never said.

RAFAL: Ah, but you do.

CAPTAIN: This one.

BORROMEO: But Cocco said the Captain ... that you hated him.

RAFAL: (*small laugh*) Cocco is sweet. You think I would dislike a man because he does not share my beliefs? Then I would hate everyone.

BORROMEO: Yes, but –

RAFAL: And the Alps. Look at them. They're so beautiful. Breathtaking, to stand naked against the sky. In the twilight I saw a stag, majestic antlers in the mist. Your cathedrals have nothing on that. Why else will a boy put vine leaves in his hair?
No, I don't hate everyone, Eminence.
But I do hate the Captain.

(*Back to the scene.*)

CAPTAIN: In fact, I have destroyed paintings. Nothing you papists need concern yourself with, though. *The Fall of the Titans. The Marriage of Bacchus and Ariadne.* Tired old irrational myths.

RAFAL: Myths?

CAPTAIN: The boy who took over the reins of the chariot of the sun –

RAFAL: Phaeton.

CAPTAIN: The sun is not a chariot. Anyone can plainly see it is an orb in the sky. It's very likely as well that our earth moves around the sun and not the other way around.

RAFAL: Oh, that's likely, is it? Who says that?

CAPTAIN: Everyone says it nowadays. Galileo.

RAFAL: Galileo?

CAPTAIN: An astronomer in Padua, who just sees what's already there.

RAFAL: But he doesn't see the gods.

CAPTAIN: No he does not.

RAFAL: He's not just destroying us, he's saying we were never there.

CAPTAIN: Passionate boy.

RAFAL: (*leaning in to the Captain*) But Captain, if the sun can't be a chariot in the sky, why not just let it be in art? Where's the harm in painted gods? They're really harmless, they can't speak. Shadows of their former selves, appealing only to a little bit of poetry, for –

CAPTAIN: Those gods are not poetry. They are old, and cold, and remote.

RAFAL: What a – ! Is the Christian god not just as remote?

CAPTAIN: The Protestant religion is not remote. The Protestants allow no one to intercede between me and the sacrifice of my Lord Jesus Christ.

RAFAL: What sacrifice?

CAPTAIN: He was crucified for our sins.

RAFAL: Oh that. That's easy. I could do that.

CAPTAIN: False gods. Dust and ashes.

RAFAL: Why you destroy paintings.

CAPTAIN: Thou shalt not make unto thee any graven image.

RAFAL: What if a graven image came to life? Then it wouldn't be old and cold –

CAPTAIN: That's impossible.

RAFAL: If some old cold god wished to make a good impression, say, on one little man, like you –

CAPTAIN: There was a goddess who made a good impression on me, as I recall.

RAFAL: Truly?

CAPTAIN: The goddess of the harvest.

RAFAL: Demeter.

CAPTAIN: So impressed was I by her beauty, I stood before her, with a little knife, sliced here, and here (*drawing a small 'x' playfully over Rafal's lips*), inserted my formidable tarse – (*laughs, shyly*)

RAFAL: You did not.

CAPTAIN: I did.

RAFAL: That could not have been so soft for you.

CAPTAIN: But this painting? Of the Virgin Mother of God? I can assure you, I feel nothing but awe before its beauty. I will protect it.

RAFAL: You admire a Virgin Mother.

CAPTAIN: Well of course.

RAFAL: You would not fuck her in the mouth. Or maybe you would, to spare her virginity.

(*The Captain is shocked. Then laughs.*)

BORROMEO: Such blasphemy.

RAFAL: Yes; such: blasphemy. I wanted to get to the castle. I wanted to see the emperor unveil the painting. I wanted the Captain to be there. I wanted him to be sorry. I wanted him to fall on his knees. I wanted him to go mad. I could hardly wait. I didn't wait. It used to be, when a man showed me disrespect, I could make him mad. Perhaps I've become a shadow of my former self, but I can still do it. I can still make a man mad. He was impressed by the sacrifice of his crucified Lord. So I showed him I could make a sacrifice too.

BORROMEO: A sacrifice?

RAFAL: I did not wait to get to Prague. And I knew ...

(*They witness the unveiling of the painting and the miracle.*)

RAFAL: Mother.

RAFAL: ... it would thwart my plan.

DOLFIN: Brilliant.

BORROMEO: Pusterwald.

COCCO: I'll be buggered.

RAFAL: But it was worth it ...

CAPTAIN: I have gone mad!

RAFAL: ... to see that man brought down ...

CAPTAIN: Forgive me I am weak!

RAFAL: ... and destroyed.

CAPTAIN: (*on his knees*) I am weak!

BORROMEO: See him destroyed how?

RAFAL: Well, he is dead, isn't he?

BORROMEO: Who?

RAFAL: The Captain. This blood on the floor? I destroyed one man and raised up another. Is this not the function of a god? To raise up the good and punish the wrongdoers? It's what we used to do, anyway, in the old days.

BORROMEO: Who did you raise up?

RAFAL: Why, did you not give preferment to Benasuto Cocco, scientist, doctor, rational man?

BORROMEO: I – How do you know that? But that had nothing to do with –

RAFAL: The function of a god.

BORROMEO: You did not raise him up. I did that!

RAFAL: As you say, Eminence.

BORROMEO: I did that! This is not evidence of your power. It is God's divine grace and my own benevolence and compassion.

RAFAL: Such self-regard.

BORROMEO: You say you need my help. And yet you mock me, employ infernal trickery and treachery, flaunt your own destructive ways and spit on me and everything I stand for.

(*Rafal falls on his face.*)

BORROMEO: Do you have a confession to make?

RAFAL: I beg you. I am nothing no more. I was only a task; and I failed it. I should go back to the stars, but now that the stars are falling, all we have left is the art. And when the art dies, the gods die.

BORROMEO: I –

RAFAL: The wreckage of just one Dionysos by Leonardo leaves me bereft, reduced, marooned.
    Eminence, have you seen the Veronese Apollo chasing Daphne?

BORROMEO: Yes.

RAFAL: She, fleeing him, caught in the moment of passionate transformation into a tree! Stone and wood and semen, the green spindle and passion –

BORROMEO: Yes.

RAFAL: – and gods.

BORROMEO: I have seen it.

RAFAL: When the art dies, the gods die. Eminence, have you seen your Correggio of the Cloud – ?

BORROMEO: I have seen it.

RAFAL: Jove embracing Io. The god is a cloud, the cloud descends, enveloping Io and you. Even though it's an image, and even though it's a cloud, it is warm.

BORROMEO: It is warm.

RAFAL: When the art dies, they die. We die. All we want is to live there. Place all the power we have left there. But there is danger there, from such destroyers as the Captain.

BORROMEO: You would stand before the emperor and have him protect your place in art.

RAFAL: Seven hills. A winding river. Winding streets. A city like the world made small. And the castle like the city made small. And the emperor: he too is small. Would he deny a god in need of help?

BORROMEO: You fear he will not believe you.

RAFAL: He would if you came with me.

BORROMEO: ...

RAFAL: Call it a miracle and come with me, Eminence. You can speak for me; you know the whole story now ... Call it a miracle, Eminence.

BORROMEO: My office cannot be conducted at your whim, my child. It is as grave an office as your own.

RAFAL: So you believe me then.

BORROMEO: What I believe –

RAFAL: One day Galileo will sweep away your god too; He will; as certain as I love a soldier.

BORROMEO: Perhaps Galileo can be swayed from his beliefs.

RAFAL: What will you put in your report?

BORROMEO: I must conclude, my child, that a miracle did not take place.

RAFAL: ... But you'll let me go to Prague?

BORROMEO: I will not report what you have done. Or believe you have done. Nor that I cannot tell whether you are a deluded boy, or a devil, or a witch, or a ...

RAFAL: Or a god, Eminence?

BORROMEO: Still, I wish you luck. Though you have no power to speak of, perhaps your passion will suffice to inspire him.

RAFAL: (*holds out his hands*) Come with me.

BORROMEO: (*shakes head*)

RAFAL: Come with me.

BORROMEO: (*shakes head*)

RAFAL: Stars, look upon this man. Here is Borromeo. Lover of art against his beliefs. Weep for him as for yourselves.

BORROMEO: Do you still have Dolfin's flask?

RAFAL: Sorry?

BORROMEO: He gave it to you, in the church, in Pusterwald. Do you still have it?

RAFAL: I have it.

BORROMEO: May I see it?

RAFAL: So small a sign would suffice?

(*Rafal hands it over. Borromeo pulls out the cork. He is interrupted by the entrance of two soldiers and Councillor Zen. The soldiers go straight to Rafal.*)

BORROMEO: Councillor, I am not finished.

ZEN: According to my notes, 'a miracle did not take place.'

BORROMEO: The walls have ears.

ZEN: You may include that fact in your full report. I'll take this young man to the dungeon.

BORROMEO: I have given my word that no harm would come to him.

ZEN: You said you would do your best. So try me.

BORROMEO: His task is worthy even if there is delusion in it. He is innocent.

ZEN: Of what? Blasphemy? Perjury? Sodomy? He has manipulated the mechanism of the Most Serene Republic for his own gain. That's good enough for me.

RAFAL: You cannot kill me. Not if he believes.

ZEN: Do you believe, Eminence?

(*Borromeo is frozen with the flask.*)

RAFAL: Did I not save your painting?

ZEN: You did. You saved a painting. And you killed a whole town.

BORROMEO: What do you mean?

ZEN: Not for your ears, Eminence. (*starts to go*)

BORROMEO: Pusterwald?

ZEN: Eminence, has anyone ever told you, your mind has a dangerous cast? You consider everything. Not only what is true and what might be true, but also what cannot be true and what should not be true.

(*Zen sweeps out with the guards and his prisoner. Borromeo is left alone, still holding the open flask. He looks at it, uncertain. Then he brings it to his lips, drinks. Pulls it away to consider the taste. His face darkens. Blackout. End of play.*)

REAPING SONG

(from Act Two, Scene Three)
Traditional Sicilian work song, arrangement by John Gzowski

ACKNOWLEDGEMENTS

The playwright gratefully acknowledges the support of the Ontario Arts Council via Crows Theatre and also the Stratford Festival's 2010 Playwrights' Retreat in the writing of the initial draft of this play.

Further thanks: George Masswohl, Martha Henry, Chris Abraham, Paul Fauteux, Michael McManus, Greg Ellwand, Johnnie Walker, Luke Humphrey, Evan Buliung, Sam Malkin, Ron Kennell, Gerold Schmidt, Richard McMillan.

And to Richard Rose, for his rigour, his challenges and his care; and to Andrea Romaldi, Andrea Donaldson, Erin Brubacher and the staff and technicians of the Tarragon Theatre, who worked so hard to make this play a reality.

ABOUT THE AUTHOR

SEAN DIXON is a playwright, novelist and actor. His plays have been produced in Canada, the U.S., Australia and the U.K., and three have been collected in *AWOL: Three Plays for Theatre SKAM*. Sean's first novel was *The Girls Who Saw Everything* (*The Last Days of the Lacuna Cabal* in the U.S. and the U.K.), named one of the Best Books of 2007 by *Quill & Quire*. His second novel was *The Many Revenges of Kip Flynn* (Coach House, 2011). He is also the author of two books for young readers, *The Feathered Cloak* and *The Winter Drey*.

Typeset in Casablanca (display font) and Goluska (text).

Goluska was designed by Canadian Rod McDonald to honour his longtime friend Glenn Goluska (1947–2011). Goluska was one of Canada's finest designers, who had a lifelong love for the work of noted American typographer William Addison Dwiggins. The typeface Goluska is an homage to Dwiggins's font Electra.

Printed at the old Coach House on bpNichol Lane in Toronto, Ontario, on Zephyr Antique Laid paper, which was manufactured, acid-free, in Saint-Jérôme, Quebec, from second-growth forests. This book was printed with vegetable-based ink on a 1965 Heidelberg KORD offset litho press. Its pages were folded on a Baumfolder, gathered by hand, bound on a Sulby Auto-Minabinda and trimmed on a Polar single-knife cutter.

Edited for the press by Heidi Waechtler and Alana Wilcox
Designed by Heidi Waechtler and Alana Wilcox
Cover detail and interior image: *Feast of the Rose Garlands* (1506), Albrecht
    Dürer. Photograph © National Gallery in Prague, 2014
Photo of Sean Dixon by Cylla von Tiedemann

Coach House Books
80 bpNichol Lane
Toronto ON M5S 3J4
Canada

416 979 2217
800 367 6360

mail@chbooks.com
www.chbooks.com